MAN-EATER

THE TERRIFYING TRUE STORY OF CANNIBAL KILLER KATHERINE KNIGHT

RYAN GREEN

For Helen, Harvey, Frankie and Dougie

Disclaimer

This book is about real people committing real crimes. The story has been constructed by facts but some of the scenes, dialogue and characters have been fictionalised.

Polite Note to the Reader

This book is written in British English except where fidelity to other languages or accents are appropriate. Some words and phrases may differ from US English.

CONTENTS

Introduction

All that Kathy ever wanted was for somebody to love her as much as she loved them.

After a brief tussle, David was on top of her again, his sweat trickling down on her as he thrust inside her over and over. All of that weight—the mechanical inevitability of each thrust and groan—was like riding a mechanical bull, except she was trying to buck it off instead of the other way around.

Did David love her? She knew that she loved him. She wouldn't be lying here, legs all twisted up at odd angles, crotch aching and insides churning with cheap beer and agonising friction if she didn't. She tried to look into his eyes, to see her love reflected back at her from inside them, but he was staring into the pillow, eyes slack and unfocused, mouth hanging open and drool pooling at the corners, clinging to the stubble of the day. There were no answers to be found in that vacant face, not after a long night at the pub.

He didn't love her the way that her father had loved her mother, all sharp words and blunt fists. She knew that for certain. David was slow with his fists, even when some fool deserved it, and he was so soft on her that it made her feel uncomfortable sometimes. He was so soft that she could push her fingers right inside him like his skin was just the skin on a pudding.

He didn't love her in the way that the little animals that she'd rescued from the roadside and nursed back to health loved her, with the unconditional adoration and terror of someone meeting their god. He wasn't obedient and cowed like an animal would be. He certainly had some animal in him, but it only came out in places like this, when his rutting and grunting and growling were somehow acceptable.

She didn't even know if he could love through the haze of booze that had been hanging around him all day. When he'd picked her up on the back of his motorbike this morning, his breath was already strong enough to strip paint. He must have spent the whole night out drinking with his buddies. One last night of freedom, he'd said. Freedom. Like she was some prison he was being sent to. Like she would ever stop him from doing what he wanted instead of helping him on his way.

Who the hell did he think he was, talking about her like she was a punishment instead of being the only good thing in his shitty, little life? How dare he make a joke out of her? She started thrashing underneath him, raking at his back with her nails. Thrusting up against him as hard as she could, desperate to throw the rotten bastard off her. He probably couldn't even feel it through the booze. All he did was make appreciative little moans.

No matter how she twisted and pushed, he just seemed to love it more—maybe this was the only way he knew how to love her, with his big meaty hands clamped on to her hips and her hair spread across the pillows. Maybe that was enough, these moments of total adoration in exchange for spreading her legs? Her mother had always told her to just go along with what men wanted to make them happy. It had been about the only good advice the old hag ever gave anybody. Kathy was tough enough to take it. She was tough enough to take on anything.

She'd proven that every day in the charnel house. Men blanched when they saw guts and blood for the first time, but Kathy took to it like a fish to water. Her knives, her precious knives, moved through that dead meat like sharks through the water, smooth and perfect, never making a ripple out of place until she wanted them to. At work, they might have feared her smart mouth a little, but they feared those knives the most. She'd offered to settle any argument or score that folks had with her by the knife and not one of them had balls big enough to try. If it were up to her, she'd carry those knives with her everywhere she went, but her fist served just as well when one of the women or, more often, men, in the pub had a wrong word to say about her and her man.

Her man. It was worth it. To be loved, to be truly loved for the very first time in her life. It was definitely worth lying back and pretending that every drop of sweat didn't sting like acid. To pretend to be as soft as he needed her to be. As soft as he was under the tough mask that he put on to impress folks.

With just a little of his blood under her fingernails, Kathy stopped clawing at him. She could do this for him, she loved him and, at the end of the day, it wasn't really all that bad. She even found she could enjoy it when she wasn't trapped inside her own head. She envied David for having it that easy; for being able to close his eyes, inhabit his body and just feel things instead of spending all his time lost in the echo chamber of his memories, repeating some snide comment that one of his cousins made about their wedding ceremony being held in a registry office, and how it was no surprise that the bride wasn't wearing white.

Had Kathy had her knives with her, she would have painted that bitch's dress red at that moment. Instead, she'd let herself get dragged along by David, twirled out onto the makeshift dance floor in the bar for their first dance together as man and wife. He'd been so drunk that he trod on her toes and let out his stupid gruff laugh when she stamped on his in return. She reached up to cup his face in her hands. He was hot to the touch. She took him upstairs.

Eyes closed and grunting with the effort. Determined to hammer her right through the bed and into the floor. The headboard of the bed was clattering against the wall with every thrust and, on their hook above the bed, Kathy's knives jangled along like a musical accompaniment to their lovemaking.

She'd had more than a few beers right alongside David tonight. She was allowed to celebrate, too—it wasn't all about him. It wasn't all about him getting to haul her eighteen-year-old ass back to bed and grunt on top of her and then go off to hoot with triumph about it to all of his stupid friends. This was what she wanted. Kathy kept repeating that to herself every time he hammered into her, every time it felt like she was going to tear in half. This was what she wanted. She wanted the husband. She wanted to have kids and settle down and do everything right, the way that her own shitty parents had never managed to. She wanted it all. She wanted to be loved.

If that love burned a little, then she would let it burn her. There were far worse fates than to be warm at night, cradled in the shelter of a big, strong body. She wanted this. She had wanted this for as long as she'd been old enough to know what a man could be to a woman. It was true enough that she could never wear a white wedding dress without lying because she'd been chasing after this love since she was old enough to run. The boys back at school had been on the receiving end of her fists a lot more often than they'd gotten under her shirt, but she put that down to being raised by a pair of bad examples. Dad's example had led her to being free with her fists and mum's example had led her to being free with her tits.

Now, she was old enough to know right and wrong for herself. Old enough to recognise that the map her parents had laid out for her led to nowhere but loneliness and misery. Her reputation might have been tarnished by her school years, but she'd swung at anyone who tried to keep her dirty when she was trying to clean herself up. David wasn't the first man she'd ever been with, not by a long shot, but he was the first one that she felt like she could trust. The first one that she gave herself to fully, instead of trying to hide inside her head when the clothes came off, the way that she had when she was a little girl.

David was getting faster and faster, his eyes still squeezed shut, even though his face was held between her hands and Kathy was kissing him with a passion that surprised even her. The jangling of the knives above them was like sleigh-bells. His breathing had a hitch in it and, for a moment, sore as she was, Kathy felt the spark of lust light up inside her. She didn't just want this. She wanted him.

She'd wanted him after the two of them staggered home together that night. She'd wanted him when he picked her up, carried her over the threshold, kicked the door shut and dumped her into the bed. Right up until the moment that he'd stripped her out of her dress and climbed on top of her for the first time, she had been electric, desperate for him and arching up into every touch. But, the moment that he was actually inside her, she vanished back inside herself. Every grunt echoed in the dark cavity of her mind, coming back louder with a dozen bad memories coming along to keep it company.

The first time they'd ever made love, she bit his lip and he'd called her a bitch, but he hadn't stopped. Just like none of the others had stopped no matter how she squealed and hollered. She'd stopped biting him now. Her old defensive instincts had grown lax. She really was getting soft.

The first time that they consummated their marriage that night, she had given him nothing harsher than kisses and he'd given her nothing gentler than the same methodical, mechanical pounding that he always did. No matter what she did, it always turned out the same.

Ten minutes after that first attempt, she'd wrapped her lips around him and started off round two with a distended grin. She knew what was expected of her as a wife. She knew that she had to let him do everything to her and she had to act like she liked it. She'd learned that much at least. If this was how he showed his love then she wanted it all. Every sweaty, painful moment of it.

This third time, she'd climbed right on top of him the minute he finished and started slithering all over him. Smearing the two of them with sweat, dragging her smooth skin over his rough hairy chest and stirring his passion up all over again. This belonged to her. This night was all about the two of them and there was no way that she was going to let it end. He couldn't turn her down. He could never turn her down. All she wanted was his love. Rejection was an impossibility. A betrayal. It had taken only three slides up and down him before he was ready to go again.

Now, it was almost over. She could feel him clenching up above her. Felt those violent thrusts get harder, deeper and slower. He let out a noise like a deflating balloon when he finished, then he rolled off her, gasping, 'I swear, keep on like this and you're going to kill me, woman.'

She lay there for a long moment letting the cold seep into her. The ache was still there between her legs, but there was a sweetness to it now, a longing. This time, when she climbed back on top of him, it wasn't just going to be for him. It was going to be for the both of them. She was going to feel whatever it was that he felt when they were making love. She was going to be complete, like the other girls got to be with their sweethearts. She was going to feel the good as well as the bad.

David's cheek bristled her when she kissed it. His breath stung her eyes as it gusted out of him in shallow puffs. His eyes were shut, but they weren't clenched shut as they'd been in the heat of the moment—his whole face was slack, even looser than the beer usually made him. She climbed on top of him and fumbled around in the soggy mess where their bodies joined. She was trying to line everything up, but David was being awkward, flopping limply in her grip in a way that he never did. She let out a little growl and jerked at him, trying to get the motor running again.

With a dirty laugh, she leaned in close to kiss him on the lips, but she stopped when he made another of his little animal noises. Not quite a grunt, not quite a breath. Her eyebrows drew down. She knew that sound. A moment later, another snore joined the second. The bastard had fallen asleep. This was her night and he was sleeping through it. He wasn't here with her. He'd shut his eyes and left her behind. He'd abandoned her. It was their wedding night and he'd fucking left her.

She untangled her hands from his nethers and took a grip on his broad shoulders instead. 'Wake up, honey.'

It took all her considerable strength to lift him and drop him back onto the mattress, but he didn't even stir. She shook him. Slapped him. Hammered her fist into his shoulder. 'Wake up, you piece of shit!'

He was still ignoring her. Still leaving her behind. Her hands slipped up over his thick-corded shoulders, trailing up his collar, leaving tracks in the cooling sweat. 'David. Wake up. Wake up! This is my wedding night! Wake up, you miserable bastard!'

Her fingers were as calloused and strong as any man's from days on the tools and when they closed around his throat they were filled with terrible anger, born from pure, blind fury. When she crushed his windpipe in that grip, his eyes finally snapped open, but by then it was too late. His blushing, beautiful bride was gone and this other Kathy—one that he didn't even know— had slipped into her place. Her face locked into a rictus of rage and hands locked around his throat.

Even his Kathy's voice was gone. This one sounded more like a growling dog than anything human. 'I'll teach you a lesson you'll never forget, you bastard.'

The Sinners

In 1949, Ken and Barbara fled their homes in Aberdeen amidst a storm of scandal.

Barbara had been married since she was a teenager to a man named Jack Roughan and they had lived together in relative peace in the sleepy Hunter's Valley town of Aberdeen. The coupling had produced four boys, two of whom were in their teenage years by the time that Barbara's infidelity was discovered.

If you wanted to work in rural Aberdeen in the 50s, your options were extremely limited. Farm work was always an option if you happened to own a farm. Mining was the alternative that most of the men fell into, though it led to a short and painful life for most men who chose that route. Leaving was an option, too, one that appealed to many of the town's youth, particularly the better-educated ones who could expect to earn a decent wage living in one of Australia's bigger cities.

For everyone else, there was the slaughterhouse. All of the local farms produced animals, animals that had to be killed and hacked up into saleable portions before being shipped out across Australia. Even by employing almost every adult in the town of Aberdeen, the workload still outstripped the manpower and they had to look further afield to keep the gory machinery turning over.

Ken Knight was a boon for the slaughterhouse's operations. He was an itinerant worker who travelled from town to town looking for work in the meat processing facilities that dotted the Australian farmlands. Whilst he had a reputation as a hard man and an even harder drinker, he was still meticulous in his work, hammering through carcass after carcass in half the time that it took his local co-workers, no matter how dire his hangover might be. It probably would have earned him the ire of his co-workers if he weren't so gregarious. They all found it extremely difficult to stay angry at Ken.

Jack Roughan was one of Ken's local co-workers and, whilst he tried to keep some distance from the man who had become the star of the slaughterhouse, they shared friends and ended up going out drinking together quite regularly—although Jack soon found that he couldn't keep up with Ken in that arena, either.

It was during those marathon binge drinking sessions that Ken met Barbara. They'd crossed paths a few times when Jack's long-suffering wife came to collect him from the pub and drag him home, but it wasn't long before the next big night out for the abattoir workers had all of their wives in attendance. There was chemistry between the two of them and Ken flirted with her all night long, right in the presence of her beer-blinded husband.

Barbara had come to hate Jack by this point in her life. He'd been her sweetheart in school, but once her teenage hormones had cooled off, she found herself trapped in a marriage with a man who honestly didn't give a damn about her. There was no women's-lib in rural Australia in the 1940s—if a wife had needs beyond those that her husband was fulfilling, then she was expected to be quiet about them until she eventually died of old age. In Ken, she saw the opportunity to rekindle her passion for life. The idea of divorce never even entered her mind; with her conservative upbringing, she knew the kind of social death that a single mother would suffer, but an affair? They were practically commonplace. The dirty little secrets that everyone gossiped about but nobody ever confronted directly. The frayed edges on the bonds of the Aberdeen community. She didn't actually want Ken so much as she longed for change and he was the only change available at the time.

At the next night out, she flirted back. Not as outrageously as Ken did—his larger than life personality provided him with the perfect cover for that sort of behaviour—but with enough vigour that he was convinced of her interest. When Jack succumbed to the liquor and a few of his friends carried him off towards home, Barbara lingered. At closing time, only Ken and Barbara were still upright. Suddenly, shyness overtook her despite all of the liquid courage that she had consumed and she tried to go home to her husband.

Ken wrapped her wrist in his massive hand and led her away, through the dull grey of the pre-dawn streets until they reached his dingy one-bedroom apartment in spitting distance of the slaughterhouse. When she was bashful, he was forceful, when she was reluctant, he was persistent.

At the next night out, the two of them ignored each other entirely. Any burgeoning suspicions that might have been hanging around their co-workers evaporated and Ken went back to winking saucily at the poor bartenders, instead. Jack kept his arm around Barbara's shoulders anyway, a little statement of ownership that didn't go unnoticed by anyone. A statement that both Barbara and Ken were happy to acknowledge. It was better if everyone knew for certain that she was Jack's wife, that she was loyal to him and had eyes for no other. The more certain everyone was of those facts, the easier it was for the two of them to sneak around behind Jack's back without interruption.

Jack and Barbara's sex life had been on the decline from the moment that it started. She was repulsed by the sexual act and had endured it exclusively for the privileges that it brought to her in the marriage. With Ken, the situation was different—sex wasn't a penance to be endured in exchange for a roof over her head and babies in her belly. It was an act of righteous rebellion.

Once she had taken up with Ken, Jack was cut off entirely. With teenage children in the house, the arguments had to be conducted quietly, but they were intense all the same. Barbara found her grocery budget slashed, her free time filled with pointless, busy work—whatever petty miseries Jack could inflict to apply pressure on her to spread her legs, he did. He grew colder and angrier with her with each passing day and every little cruelty just reinforced Barbara's suspicion that all he had ever cared about was sex. He didn't love her. He didn't even pretend to help with taking care of their children anymore. Their marriage was a hollowed-out husk and she was bone-tired of pretending otherwise.

Things were at boiling point and all that it took to tip things over was a bruise on her thigh that looked like a handprint, if you squinted. Jack went mad. He beat Barbara until she was covered in bruises and threw her out of the house. Tossing her limited wardrobe out into the mud with her.

Whilst other cuckolded men in Aberdeen had the sense to keep things quiet, to prevent the shame and scrutiny that this sort of betrayal brought down on a family, Jack was too enraged to care. Within a day, all one thousand five hundred people living in the little town knew that his wife had been unfaithful.

The identity of the man that she had been having her affair with wasn't yet known, but it didn't take long before Barbara was found. Homeless and destitute, she had turned to the only person in Aberdeen who she was certain wouldn't turn her away or beat her even worse than Jack had. She moved into Ken's tiny apartment the same day she was thrown out of her family home.

The rumours about the two of them abounded and, before long, their shame was the talk of the whole town. Barbara's own children wouldn't even look her in the eye. The two younger boys had been shipped off to live with Jack's sister in Sydney, two hundred miles away, without Barbara even being informed. The two older boys sided with their father, going so far as to spit at their mother in the street when they saw her. The words 'whore' or, more politely, 'adulteress,' dogged her footsteps everywhere that she went.

With nothing left to tie her to Aberdeen, Barbara begged Ken to take her away. With only a pair of suitcases, the two headed off across New South Wales to find themselves a new place to call home. A place where nobody knew the shameful secret that had started their union.

They found that place in the town of Moree and he easily found work in the local slaughterhouse with the same jovial manner and practiced hands that had won him pride of place in Aberdeen society. Through letters and only a single court appearance, Barbara was able to secure her divorce from Jack Roughan, returning to her maiden name of Thorley for only a week before a hasty registry office ceremony branded her as Ken Knight's property, instead.

Whilst Barbara had lost all of her friends and contact with most of her family, the Knights were still a presence in Moree and they didn't care what circumstances had led their prodigal son back to them—they were just happy to have him nearby again. Their rapidly arranged wedding was conducted with Ken's locally famous brother, Oscar, as the best man and a few other family members as witnesses. Barbara was already beginning to show signs of her first pregnancy of the new marriage by the time that the ink was dry on the marriage licence.

Two boys were born in the years that followed, new sons to replace those that Barbara had lost when her first marriage disintegrated. Instead of chasing after the change she had so desperately craved, she instead found herself sinking further and further into an identical rut. The only difference was that this time, cold, angry looks were far from the only punishment she received for breaking away from her wifely duties.

Ken had always been an alcoholic, but amidst the hard-drinking culture of rural Australia, it wasn't immediately apparent that it was a problem rather than just another aspect of his gregarious personality. In isolation, with only Barbara and toddlers for company, it became immediately obvious that it was not merely a source of distraction but a crippling addiction. There was not a single day that passed without Ken getting so drunk he was slurring his speech. The good money that he made working in the local abattoir was whittled away in local bars before the family even got a chance to spend it on essentials. Whilst Barbara might have felt like a prisoner in a gilded cage with Jack, when she was with Ken, that cage began to tarnish and show its true colours.

Once again, she started to fantasise about how she might make her escape—eyeing the other men in Ken's life with an appraising eye and finding that none of them wanted anything to do with her. Ken's reputation preceded him in Moree and nobody wanted to cross the man, or his family, by getting involved in an affair. Painfully aware that a divorce could only end in her losing her precious children all over again, Barbara prepared to hunker down and endure the marriage with as little contact with Ken as was physically possible.

Ken did not respond well to the withdrawal of her affections. His sexual appetites had almost been a running joke back when they lived in Aberdeen and Barbara had adored the passion when they were still in their courtship phase. But, now that they were married, his ardour had not cooled even a little. He demanded sex constantly, sometimes as often as ten times a day. When Barbara refused him, he did not shy away as her first husband had. At first, he would beat her into compliance. Then, when even that began to fail, he simply forced himself on her.

Barbara was trapped in the house with two little boys, raped as often as ten times a day, beaten for every slight infraction against the rules that her new iron-fisted tyrant of a husband laid down. She might have escaped her nightmare life of boredom and mediocrity back in Aberdeen, but she had plunged headlong into a fresh hell of her own making; a poster-child for the puritanical beliefs about the sanctity of marriage that held sway at the time.

Her children were the only light in her life, but it didn't take long before both of her precious boys were learning the lessons that their father imparted through his actions as much as his words. By the time that they were walking, they were throwing punches at one another and at their mother. They treated their father with the respect that he considered his due, but their mother was little more than a slave to their whims. Alone and surrounded by vicious men and vicious men in training, Barbara longed for any sort of help against the tide of evil that surrounded her.

When she discovered that she was pregnant again, at the start of 1955, all of the usual delight that that discovery would have brought had been beaten out of her. The discovery that she was carrying twins just made things so much worse. There would be five of them. Five men, demanding and tormenting her, night and day. Stripping away whatever distant hope of escape that she might have harboured.

Imagine her delight when, on the 24th October 1955, she gave birth to a pair of non-identical twin girls in Tenterfield, New South Wales. Beautiful baby girls with her Irish red hair already curling on their foreheads. Allies.

Daddy's Girl

The younger of the two girls was named Katherine and the older twin, Joy.

Joy adapted quickly to life in a house full of masculine energy, becoming a tomboy and allying herself with the men against Barbara. Katherine quickly became her mother's only hope and only confidante.

She was a pretty little girl and she spent a great deal of her time playing with dolls and dresses. Despite his less than conservative actions, Ken was a conservative at heart. He deeply approved of his daughter behaving in what he considered to be 'feminine' ways and, whilst he treated his wife with utter contempt, considering her to be little more than a tool for his pleasure, in little Katherine he found—if not a kindred spirit—at least a balm to the hypermasculinity of his work environment, persona and lifestyle. Katherine was a quiet place that he could visit, where there was no judgement, no competition, no frustration and no backbiting, just the unconditional love of a girl who viewed her father as something akin to God.

But, if Ken was God, then he was the vengeful Old Testament version. He demanded obedience and compliance, not only from his battered sex doll but also from the children. The boys were raucous and rebellious, with nobody around who could control them all day long. Their only authority figure had literally and figuratively been stripped of all dignity in front of them far too often for them to listen to a word Barbara said, and the end result of Ken's brand of discipline tended to be bruises rather than life lessons.

Joy fell in with the boys, joining in their vicious games, but Katherine always held herself apart. She wasn't the most obedient child, but when she was stubborn, Ken looked on it as a virtue rather than a sign of defiance. He beat her with a dog leash when she was disobedient, switching to an extension cord when he was feeling generous or when he couldn't remember where he'd left the leash after his last drunken fury.

Whilst the other children received the same beating over and over, Katherine was a little quicker to adapt her behaviour. She was still the recipient of a great many unwarranted beatings throughout her young life, but they were rarely for the same reason twice. She was soft and pliant when he needed her to be and tough and rough when he wanted her to stand up for herself. She modelled herself on him and the ally that Barbara had been so desperately hoping for was co-opted by the enemy.

Barbara didn't take the loss well. She'd brought two daughters into the world after two awful marriages and both of them had turned against her in their own ways. She sunk into an even deeper depression, withdrawing entirely from the world, going through the motions of motherhood without seeking out any emotional connections or joy and enduring Ken's ever more violent violations with a cold stoicism born of total disassociation.

Her only small recompense was company. Katherine may have looked on her mother as too weak to defend herself, but she didn't overlook the woman's value as a teacher. It didn't take long before Katherine graduated from playing house with her dolls to trying to take over the running of the real household. She learned everything that she could about housekeeping, cooking and sewing from her mother. By the time she was old enough to turn the knobs on the stove, Katherine was already supplanting her mother in the kitchen, just as she'd supplanted her in Ken's affections.

As the girls got older, Barbara began talking to Katherine as though she were her confidante, even though Katherine had given her no reason to place her trust in her. Ultimately, she had nobody to tell. She was just as isolated as Barbara by their living situation and, with no basis for comparison, she assumed that every mother spoke to her daughters in the same way. Sharing explicit sexual details, ranting and complaining about all of the misery that had befallen her and sharing all of the sordid family secrets that Katherine would soon become the keeper of.

Rural Australia was not the most progressive place in the late 50s and the racism that the aboriginal people suffered on a daily basis made even America's civil rights history look positively heart-warming. Even the suspicion of aboriginal ancestry was enough to get a family marked as social pariahs. Whilst Barbara's Irish great-grandfather granted both her and her children their distinctive red hair—and a good deal of the European features that helped to disguise their true ancestry— her great-grandmother had been an indigenous Australian. Two generational infusions of white heredity had helped to mask the family's appearance, but as Barbara's sanity continued to decline, she began obsessing more and more over that ancestry, taking pride in being different from the men who abused her.

She taught her daughters about their aboriginal ancestry, making sure to instil the requisite fear of exposure in them. She had meant for it to bring them together as a family, but all it did was layer more pressure onto an already tense situation. Now, the girls believed that society outside of their immediate family was against them, that no assistance would be forthcoming even if they did eventually reach out for help. Their ancestry became another lock on the cage that kept them trapped inside the nightmarish Knight family.

As if the pressure in the Knight household wasn't already high enough, things worsened yet again in 1959, when Katherine was only four-years-old. Jack Roughan died and the two older boys who had been living with him were passed into the care of their mother. Already in their teenage years and suffering from a nasty shock after the death of their father, the boys submerged themselves entirely in the culture of their new family. If Barbara had hoped that the presence of the older boys might calm her new brood of hellions, she was wrong. The older boys had lost all respect for their 'whore' of a mother when she abandoned them back in Aberdeen and they were almost gratified to see how badly she was being treated. Some of this was idolisation of their lost father, but no small part was simply adaptation to their surroundings. Nobody else cared about Barbara, why should they?

If their contempt had extended only as far as their mother, then their contribution to the darkness that was gathering in the Knight household would have been negligible. Unfortunately, they swiftly learned from the example of their adoptive father and began to look at all women as disposable sex toys with no agency of their own: an example that was constantly reinforced by their peers and the other men in the community in more subtle ways than Ken's barbaric displays of dominance. Girls their own age had protections in place—the cultural expectation that they would wait until marriage, accompanied by the overbearing threat of violence from the girls' fathers and a whole whisper network to keep them from being left alone with boys like the 'new Knight kids.' All it took was a few fumbling attempts at molestation before the Roughan boys were blacklisted from every social event in town and every girl was given fair warning that they were after their virtue.

With no outlets for their burgeoning sexuality and no privacy within the family home due to the sheer volume of boys crammed into each room, they soon started looking a little closer to home for release. Joy was spared their attention thanks to her being 'one of the guys,' but the more feminine Katherine soon became the focal point for both of the older boys' sexual awakenings.

Between the ages of four and fourteen, Katherine was the target of a gradually worsening series of sexual assaults in her own home. A campaign of molestation that started with friendly touching, cuddles and gentle innocent kisses, gradually transformed into games where Katherine was stripped of her clothes and her dignity. As they grew old enough, the younger duo also started to join in with their new brothers' favourite hobby. Before she had even reached her teenage years, all four boys were using her for their sexual pleasure. If it hadn't been for her mother's example, Katherine would have been mystified by the strange actions of the boys, but Barbara was always more than happy to regale her girls with tales of her sexual exploitation, giving them all the explicit details of the 'disgusting' things that men would want them to do.

Katherine finally had the courage to ask, 'What do you say if you don't want to do those things?'

Her mother gave her the worst advice she would ever receive in her life. 'Just let them do what they want with you. It's easier that way.'

With that in mind, Katherine never reported her brothers' escalating sexual behaviour, even as they moved on to frottage and exploring her body outside the confines of the games that they'd played when she was young enough to believe they were only games. Just as Barbara became the receptacle of all Ken's sexual frustrations, so too did Katherine suffer that same fate— never speaking out and never truly knowing whether her life was normal or hellish.

As she grew older, Katherine began to seek out safe avenues of escape from her home life. Whilst she had no way of knowing that other families were not enveloped in the same maelstrom of chaos, she had found a few safe shelters outside of it. In particular, she discovered that she loved spending time with her Uncle Oscar.

In his youth, Oscar had been a champion horseman, famous in New South Wales for his skills and, whilst he had been forced to abandon that career as age wore away his competitive edge, he still maintained a horse farm where he tended to both his old champions and rescue horses that had been abandoned or abused. Katherine fit right in. She spent as much time as possible with Oscar, helping to care for the horses and any other animal that she found at the farm. Whilst her father's interactions with nature mainly involved butchering it, Oscar taught Katherine to love animals as more than just a resource.

Before long, she was rescuing injured animals and nursing them back to health in her room at home. She was fiercely defiant when Ken tried to take them away from her, to the point that she was able to make the brutal patriarch back down and let her tend to her wounded birds in peace. When she found larger animals in need of help, she called on Oscar and he took as many as possible into his stables or passed them along to a veterinarian who could provide the creatures with the care they required or the tender mercy of an overdose.

Oscar was a landmark in her life, a point that she could have used to navigate a new course. One where she didn't follow in her father's footsteps. One where the brutality of her home life was a distant memory instead of her daily reality. But, sadly, Oscar had his own struggles in life. Despite the brave face that he put on for Katherine, he was riddled with depression and in 1969, when she was only fourteen years old, he took his own life, turning the gun that he had used to put down so many injured horses on himself and putting an end to his own misery for once.

This was the breaking point for Katherine. The moment when all of the rage and misery that she had dammed up inside herself throughout her life finally cracked the veneer of good behaviour that her father had demanded. The next time one of her brothers tried to feel her up, she punched him so hard she nearly broke his jaw and threatened to castrate him the next time that he laid a hand on her. It was like a switch had been flipped, like a different person had just started to inhabit her body.

After the boy had fled to his brothers with this tale, the older boys approached Katherine and discovered that she was in just as good a temper as always, cheerful and charming despite her current state of upset. They discounted the younger boy's story as a misunderstanding. Over the next months, both of the older boys would suffer minor, yet painful, stab-wounds that they would blame on accidents in the kitchen. One of them walked around sporting a black eye that he claimed to have acquired rough-housing with his younger siblings in an accident.

None of them dared to talk about what Katherine had become capable of because that would lead to a conversation about what had pushed her so far over the edge. Even if the younger boys and girls had no knowledge of the world outside their walls, the older boys knew perfectly well what happened to rapists in rural communities like Moree and Aberdeen. There were plenty of farms around with plenty of the rubber tubes and scissors used for quick-and-dirty castrations on troublesome beasts. It is safe to say that, in those days, in those communities, there were very few repeat offenders.

After the death of Oscar, life in Moree began to sour for the Knight family. He had been their closest tie to the community and his minor celebrity status had helped to shield his brother from any criticism that his abnormal lifestyle and 'sinful' choices might have brought him. The people that knew Ken, outside of his family, all considered him to be a lovable rogue, but the community at large didn't have to contend with his personality when trying to disapprove— they only had to deal with the concept of him. After more than a decade in their new home, the old rumours about Barbara and her previous husband had finally caught up to them and it was as if the scandal had happened only yesterday.

Meanwhile, Barbara's family back in Aberdeen had started to soften in their stance towards her without the daily visual reminder of her sins in the form of the Roughan boys running through town. She had begun communicating with them through rather stilted letters, knowing them well enough to realise that they would never help her escape the fresh hell she had gotten herself into, but hoping that one positive relationship in her life, untainted by Ken's lust, might be a tether to hold her sanity together.

When the situation in Moree became untenable, it took very little prompting on her part to have the whole family relocate yet again, this time fleeing not further from the site of their original sin, but back to the scene of the crime. By the time Katherine was fifteen, they were settled back in Aberdeen, the town she'd consider home for the rest of her adult life.

Life on the Borderline

For the first year after their return to Aberdeen in 1969, Katherine had to catch the bus to Muswellbrook High School every day to complete her state-mandated education. She was an unknown element to the children of Aberdeen and so they began to test her, to find out what this new arrival was made of.

As it turned out, she was made out of harder stuff than the farm boys that took it into their heads to torment her. After only a week, the usual 'new kid' bullying on the school bus ground to a halt out of safety concerns. Katherine was polite and charming so long as nothing riled up her temper, but once someone had crossed her, it was like a switch flipped. She would defend herself readily against any insult using her fists, boots or cutting remarks, going well beyond the level of retribution that her would-be bullies might have expected, and into the territory of vendettas. Days after a girl tried to trip her as she walked up the bus aisle, Katherine came up behind her and snipped off her braided ponytail with a pair of scissors. When a boy made a lewd comment about her early-developing breasts, she responded by smashing his teeth against the back of the seat in front of him.

For as long as Katherine was enraged, the bus became a war zone, but when her teachers confronted her later, they were unable to align the stories that they were told about her behaviour with the polite, friendly and cheerful girl that sat before them. For the first six months, the burden of proof fell on her victims and even they had to admit that she had been provoked into her behaviour, even if that behaviour was completely out of proportion when compared to the minor slights it was in response to.

Having established herself as someone who was not to be messed with, Katherine settled into the educational routine. Even at fifteen, she still had only the most basic reading and writing skills, but in this, she wasn't drastically different from many of the children around her and what she lacked in polish, she made up for in ingenuity.

She was frequently at the top of her class, despite her academic shortcomings. Even the children who expected to go on to higher education and careers outside of farming, children who studied and worked hard, would struggle to surpass her. To the vast majority of her teachers, she was a model student. But, it didn't take long before her savage temper took its toll on her reputation and the lives of others there, too.

Bullying was common enough at the school—an extreme form of peer pressure that helped to instil conservative values in those children who were straying too far from the straight and narrow path of normalcy and stoicism that their community demanded of them. But, even in a school where insults and violence were the norm, Katherine was considered to take it too far, terrorising the younger children who had crossed her, to the point of tears on a daily basis. To her peers, she was to be respected, but to those in the lower classes, she was the bogeyman. All that a child had to do was get on her bad side and then their life would become hell. At least, until her dark mood had passed.

Even her ridiculous bullying behaviour was overlooked as a part of the normal school experience until the day that she stabbed one of her victims for the terrible crime of talking back to her. The knife that she used was small enough to hide in the folded-over top of her skirt, ready at hand whenever her foul temper demanded it, but close enough to her private parts that none of the almost entirely male staff would dare to go searching for it if word ever got back to them about it. Even when they were confronted with a bleeding young boy screaming on the hallway floor with Katherine standing over him, her excellent reputation among the staff protected her from consequences beyond a letter home about her behaviour. The teachers never found the knife that she had used. They barely even looked for it.

When Ken read that letter, slowly, using a finger to track his position in the text, he asked Katherine if her victim had deserved it and her answer of 'yes' was enough to satisfy him that justice had been done. If anything, he was proud of his favourite daughter for standing up for herself. Ken was trapped in the usual position of the overbearing patriarch. To him, all women were nothing more than property, but in the case of his daughter, she was his property. Property that he wasn't around to defend at all times. He wanted her to be subservient to both him and men in general, but also to defend herself against the dangers that other men, like him, would present to her.

She probably would have made it through her whole school career with her standing in the community unscathed if it hadn't been for the one fateful day that her favourite teacher gave her a bad grade.

Katherine had been quiet all the way through the class, staring sullenly down at the papers in front of her as if she were back to struggling through them like she had when she first arrived. Her teacher kept glancing over at her; the cheerful girl who usually bounced to her feet every time that he asked the class a question, had fallen silent and still. He wondered if perhaps she'd taken ill or was suffering from what the other teachers called 'woman's troubles.' He didn't want to pry if it was the latter—he knew more about that subject than he cared to already—but if she was actually ill, he wanted to see that she was taken care of.

'Kathy? You all right, love?'

She didn't even look up at him. Her hands were in her lap and she was fidgeting around. Maybe it was woman's troubles. He groaned internally. That was the last thing he needed today. Blood all over his classroom. The girls from town were all right, but some of this country lot, they'd make the whole place look like a slaughterhouse before they thought to put a stopper in it. Kathy had never let on about this sort of trouble before, but he'd heard enough from girlfriends through the years to know that things could change on you.

'Kathy, you weren't saying much today. Is something the matter?'

Her head snapped up. 'Is something the matter?' she snapped back, 'What do you think?'

She threw the loose papers at his face and they fluttered uselessly to the floor. 'Is something the matter? You're meant to be on my side. You're meant to help me. Why'd you fail me? Eh? You've just been leading me along all this time. Making me think you're on my side when really you just want to spit on me like those other pigs.'

She flung herself out of her seat and instinct kicked in. He backpedalled rapidly. Hands flung up in supplication. 'Calm down, Kathy. It is just one test. You'll have plenty of chances to make up for ... '

'Don't you tell me to calm down,' she snarled. 'You're just like the others. You never cared about me.'

He was still backing away. She was still advancing with the inevitability of the tides. 'Kathy, it was just one test! It doesn't matter.'

She roared. 'You don't matter, you cunt-faced son of a whore.'

His eyes widened. He'd heard rumours about Katherine's foul temper and foul mouth, but he'd never expected that he or any other teacher would be on the receiving end.

'Now, steady on. You can't talk to me like that!'

'Fuck you!' Her arm drew back and, for the first time, he saw the shimmer of steel in her hand.

'Kathy, no!'

He sidestepped the first stab, otherwise, it would have gone right into his gut. He danced back across the whole classroom with her in pursuit; his legs banged into his desk. He had nowhere left to run.

She slashed at him, tearing a ragged line through his leisure suit and his shirt but narrowly missing flesh.

'Kathy, stop!'

He tried to grab at her wrist and nearly lost his fingertips for his trouble. Her eyes were glazed over. Drool was flecking on her lips and her pretty little face locked in a rictus of fury. She couldn't hear a word he was saying through the roaring of blood in her ears.

Katherine drew the knife back and he then realised the truth. She wasn't going to stop. She was going to keep going until she killed him.

Instinct saved him again. Fight or flight. Before, his body had moved without thought to get him out of the way of the danger. Now, the other half of that survival instinct prevailed.

His fist lashed out and caught Katherine under the chin. She was strong for a fifteen-year-old girl, stronger than any of her peers, thanks to the manual labour she had done at home and at her uncle's farm, but, for all of that, she was a teenage girl and he was a grown man. When he hit her, it lifted her right off her feet.

She landed on her back, the wind knocked out of her and the vacant stare more likely caused by shock than frenzy. As soon as she managed to gulp air into her lungs, she started sobbing. Wailing. Loud enough for everyone in the building to hear and come running.

'Oh god, Kathy, I'm so sorry. Are you alright?'

He dropped down beside her. He just couldn't help himself. Even now he only wanted to help her. It was just luck that he knelt on top of the knife, and her hands found only corduroy instead of another opportunity to make herself a murderer. The student body pressed in at the door and it felt like an eternity before another teacher managed to wade through them and take in the scene.

'My god. What did you do?'

The teacher was suspended from the school following the incident, as was Katherine, but whilst he was wreathed in suspicion and contempt, she was allowed to play the victim, suspended from school to recover from the traumatic event. An investigation was carried out by the school board—people who had no direct interaction with Katherine—and suddenly the picture of her abusive behaviour came into stark relief.

The teacher was reinstated with back pay and an apology and Katherine was allowed back only under probation. She served out the last month of school in a silent cloud of rage, never once interacting with the man she had tried to kill and barely keeping her foul temper in check with the other members of staff. Without a constant stream of praise to sustain her, she left school at fifteen years old with no qualifications.

This became an established pattern throughout Katherine's life, a pattern that psychologists and criminologist clung to as an explanation for her erratic behaviour. She would eventually be diagnosed with borderline personality disorder (BPD), which explained many of these strange habits away.

Those afflicted with BPD suffer from emotional instability— in Katherine's case, almost always caused by feelings of rejection or abandonment. They suffer from cognitive distortions, where they see the world in black and white, with anyone who isn't actively 'with them' being considered an enemy. They are also prone to catastrophising, where they make logical leaps from minor impediments in their plans to assumptions of absolute ruin.

BPD is often characterised by extremely intense but unstable relationships, as the sufferer gives everything that they can to a relationship in their attempts to ensure their partner never leaves but instead end up burning themselves out and blaming that same partner for the emotional toll that it takes on them.

The final trait of BPD is impulsive behaviour, often characterised as self-destructive behaviour. In Katherine's case, this almost always manifested itself in her hair-trigger temper. When she was enraged, it was like she lost all rational control over her actions, seeing everyone else as her enemies. This manifested itself in the ridiculous bullying she conducted at school, in her lashing out when she failed her test and in the vengeance that she took on her sexual abusers. It is likely that she inherited this disorder from her mother, who showed many of the same symptoms, and that they were exacerbated by her chaotic home life and the lack of healthy relationships in the adults around her that she might have modelled herself after.

With Katherine, it was like a Jekyll and Hyde switch took place when her temper was raised. The charming, eager-to-please girl who usually occupied her body was replaced with a furious, foul-mouthed hellion bent on exacting her revenge no matter what the cost. In itself, this could have been an excellent excuse for almost everything that she did wrong in her life, up to and including the crimes that she would later be accused of. Unfortunately, this sort of 'flipped switch' argument doesn't hold up when you consider that her choice to arm herself with a lethal weapon was premeditated. Part of this may certainly have been the cognitive distortion that Katherine experienced, telling her that everyone else was out to get her and that she had to defend herself, but ultimately, she was choosing to give a weapon to a person who would use it to end lives, if she had the opportunity. Assuming that this division of personalities actually existed, then 'good' Katherine was an accomplice to 'bad' Katherine, giving her the material support and planning that she needed to commit her vicious attacks.

Of course, all of this is predicated on the idea that Katherine actually suffered from BPD. It is entirely possible that there was no imbalance in her brain chemistry that made her behave in the way that she did. That, if anything, her outlook on life was based entirely on the example relationships that she had experienced during her childhood, providing a roadmap for her entire future. The Knight household was home to the sort of dog-eat-dog anarchy that would prompt rational people to violently defend themselves, perhaps even making pre-emptive moves against potential abusers.

After her diagnosis of BPD in later life, the medication that was provided to Katherine never seemed to have its intended effect. No matter how high the dosage she received, psychopharmacology failed to inhibit her violent outbursts and twisted worldview. Casting the accuracy of this diagnosis even further into doubt was the fact that many of the psychiatrists who studied Katherine in later life did not agree with the diagnosis, whilst she herself clung to it as a defence against having to take responsibility for her actions.

Whenever Katherine was accused of wrongdoing throughout her life, she would go through the same patterns to defend herself. First, she would deny that her crime had ever been committed. Then, she would deny that she was responsible. When both of those failed, her final fall-back position was always that the person whom she had victimised had deserved the punishment. BPD offered her one final out; even if her victim didn't deserve whatever the latest cruelty was that Katherine had conjured up, it still wasn't her fault. It was her sickness.

Katherine's first port of call following the ignominious end to her educational career was the Aberdeen slaughterhouse. She went in with her father, first thing in the morning before the sun had even risen, so that she could beg for a job—any job. Her lifelong dream had been to follow in her father's footsteps and work the meat line. She had been studying the swift actions of his hands since she was old enough to remember, mesmerised by the way that the blades of his boning knives danced in his strangely delicate grasp. In her limited world, her father was a god and, in the community that surrounded them, that God was worshipped for his mastery of the knife.

The shift manager at the abattoir took one look at the waifish redhead and told her no, that it wasn't work suited to a woman and that she'd be better suited looking for work elsewhere. Thanks to the presence of Ken in the building, Katherine was able to keep her temper in check, otherwise, the polite conversation might have turned foul, very quickly.

Still, her dreams of living by the blade never left her. She found another factory job in one of the only other places in town, a clothing manufacturer, where it was her job to cut the fabric to size. She had considerable experience with clothes-making by this point in her life. Almost all of her own clothes were handmade; she'd been handling repairs on her brothers' forever torn trousers for as long as she'd been able to hold a needle and Barbara had gradually been ceding territory to her in regard to Ken's clothing, too. By keeping to herself and focusing on the work, she soon found that she excelled in her new role, earning considerable praise from her employers. With the fair wage she was earning there, she was able to move out of her parents' home and into a small apartment in town, near to the factory. It was the first time in her life that she was free to come and go as she pleased and it didn't take long before she realised that this pleased her very much.

The other women in the factory weren't exactly subdued, but they were a far cry from the sort of company that Katherine wanted, so, before long, she got into the habit of heading across town to drink with the slaughterhouse workers after her shift ended.

She became well-known among them for her foul mouth and ready fists. It took barely any time at all before the man who would have been her supervisor revised his opinion of whether she was too ladylike to work among the blood and guts. In terms of violence and grotesque language, she could hold her own with the men. Stories about her incredible work ethic, prowess with the knives and manual dexterity spread out of the factory and through the gossip network to reach the ears of the married men at the slaughterhouse. The only group at the slaughterhouse who wouldn't have been singing her praises were the single men and, as it turned out, Katherine's other hedonistic behaviour soon tackled that. It wasn't that she was loose with her affections. Quite the opposite, she went after each individual man with a hunger akin to desperation. A longing that they often found off-putting, rather than flattering.

Regardless of that one questionable habit, when she turned sixteen, Katherine went back to the slaughterhouse and asked for a second time about a job and, with the credentials that she had established in her year living alone, it was impossible for them to refuse her. So, in 1971, she turned in her notice at the factory and started work at her 'dream job' in the Aberdeen slaughterhouse, cutting up offal for dog food.

For Whom the Wedding Bells Toll

Katherine had always known that she would excel in the abattoir, but even she couldn't have predicted her meteoric rise. It soon became apparent to everyone just how skilled she was with her tools and, within a few weeks, they began testing her on more complex jobs around the slaughterhouse. She bounced from one production line to the next, proving her mastery of each job before being upgraded to an even more complex task the following week. This grand tour of the slaughterhouse gave her a chance to make the acquaintance of nearly every man who worked there and she most assuredly left an impression.

Those men who hadn't crossed her path before were in for a nasty shock when they tried to treat her like a girl. The first time someone on the line raised his voice to her, she quietly and politely offered to settle their disagreement with their 'fucking knives.' A suggestion that would arise regularly throughout her time in the slaughterhouse. Nobody was ever foolish enough to take her up on the offer. They'd all seen her work.

It wasn't long before she started to relax and come out of her shell, joining in with the foul-mouthed banter and establishing herself as a force to be reckoned with socially, as well as physically. Still, she continued to bounce around the abattoir until 1972 when she finally arrived at what was widely considered to be the most complex and demanding task on the line: deboning. It was the job that had made her father's reputation and she ended up working alongside him when their shifts aligned. Ken hadn't become lax as the years went by, but he had achieved a certain level of excellence and then plateaued. Now, there was suddenly a new competitor for the throne and he was forced to push himself harder and work faster to stay ahead of the girl nipping at his heels.

For Katherine's part, she didn't even seem to be aware that she was competing. All of her life she had been waiting to get this job and now she was simply doing everything in her power to keep it. If one of the other men had surpassed Ken in his work, he probably would have accepted it as an inevitable part of his advancing years, but to see a teenage girl coming for his crown was disheartening—even if it was his own daughter who had trained at his elbow for years. They never argued about it, never even spoke about it. Ken worked harder than he ever had in his life and his example was an inspiration to Katherine, who worked all the harder to try to keep up with him.

The owners of the business weren't blind to the incredible work being done under their roof, or the way that Katherine's presence was driving all of her co-workers on to greatness. Efficiency in the slaughterhouse went up wherever Katherine went and it wasn't just her direct contribution. None of the other men wanted to be shown up by her and, once they had been, they strove even harder to try to wash that shame away.

With these deliberate and accidental contributions in mind, the owners of the slaughterhouse felt like they needed to reward Katherine, not with anything as dangerously disruptive as a pay rise, but with some little reminder that she was appreciated.

Exactly one year on from her first day in the slaughterhouse, she was gifted with her very own set of personalised knives and a leather bag to carry them around in. She carried them with her to work every day from then on, honing their edge to razor sharpness and proudly displaying them on a hook above her bed when she was at home. They were her prized possession. A trophy and testament to her skill in the only area of her life where she'd ever felt truly valued.

The owners of the slaughterhouse would never have asked Katherine to serve as any sort of example, but her natural inclinations were sufficient to have her parading around the slaughterhouse, even on her days off. She liked to visit all of the different parts of the process, chat with the men about their work and watch them at their tasks.

Her absolute favourite place in the entire production line was the pig room. She would spend every lunch hour lingering there and chatting away with the old man who had the unenviable duty of killing the pigs in full view of the others in the pen. Whilst the cattle were typically slaughtered with a stunning blow to the head before the knife-work began, the smaller creatures were not afforded the same kindness. Their wailing squeals could be heard throughout the entire building over the course of the day. High-pitched, shrill and almost human-sounding screams. Katherine was fascinated. There were a lot of foul rumours circulating about the old man who slaughtered the pigs, mainly revolving around the fact that he enjoyed his work more than was appropriate and because of this he lived a fairly lonely life, with the exception of his new best friend Katherine, in whom he found something of a kindred spirit.

In his desperation to keep her engaged, it wasn't long before he began breaking the rules, killing the pigs in front of her in increasingly cruel and elaborate ways. Once, even skinning a whole pig in front of her whilst it was still alive and screaming. Even that wasn't enough for Katherine. She didn't just want to watch, she wanted to participate.

At first, he would let her step in and deliver the lethal killing cut to the throat—spraying arterial blood all over her waterproofed apron as she cackled with glee. But soon even that wasn't sufficient to keep her entertained. She would chase a pig around the enclosure, seeing how many cuts she could inflict before it fell down dead, snipping a ligament here and a muscle there to see how far she could twist the pig's movements whilst still keeping it fleeing from her in terror. She had transformed from the little girl who tried to save roadkill and nurse it back to health into a gleeful torturer of animals.

The full extent of Katherine's lunch-break activities obviously weren't known to the owners, who wouldn't have approved of the risk of meat getting spoiled by her antics, but the other workers seemed to be thoroughly aware of her sadistic capacity for cruelty and the stories about what she did to the pigs were sufficient to keep even those who doubted the threat that she posed, in line.

Despite all of the positive attention that Katherine was getting for her 'one of the boys' attitude and workplace achievements, she was on the receiving end of just as many romantic overtures from the majority male workforce that she spent every waking hour with. She headed straight from work to the pub with the rest of the men—following after her father's example in that respect, too— although she differed greatly in the fact that she didn't actually drink alcohol, faking her way through every single night with the assistance of the bar staff and a substantial amount of lemonade. Outside of work, she allowed her more feminine side to show, behaving more like the country-girl that the abattoir workers were accustomed to courting and beginning to garner attention now that she wasn't so desperately pursuing them.

She had an ongoing flirtation with an older man named John Chillingworth, but he was perturbed by the age difference between them. Despite being an alcoholic in the truest sense, he was never quite inebriated enough to take up the seventeen-year-old girl's offers to take him home with her. Some part of that may have been the looming presence of her intimidating father in the background of every conversation that they had, or perhaps it was simply an instinct for self-preservation. After all, Chillingworth had been one of the few men to press a workplace argument with Katherine beyond the shouting stage until she drew her knives on him. He had caught a glimpse of the madness behind her mask of civility and, whilst the wildness of Katherine might have intrigued him, he wasn't willing to risk his reputation as a decent man in the community by chasing some teenager, no matter how pretty or exciting she might be.

Still, for every cautious man like John Chillingworth, there were plenty of fools like David Kellett, who couldn't see underneath the paper-thin veneer of a pretty, young girl to the darkness inside.

Aberdeen was verging on being a company town for the abattoir employees, with terraced houses constructed by the owners of the 'meat-works' to provide low-cost barracks for all of their employees around the slaughterhouse itself. It was a good few streets away before you came upon property that wasn't under the Australian Meat Cutting and Freezing Company's jurisdiction, and a few streets more before you hit upon the commercial property that usually surrounded the hubs of industry like the abattoir. The town of Aberdeen had only two licensed establishments where alcohol could be purchased and consumed—a bar and a hotel—and both of them were sensibly situated in easy walking distance of the slaughterhouse, just beyond that line of demarcation between company property and the town proper.

The bar was usually the preference for the line workers and the hotel was preferred by management, though there was a lot of crossover as almost every man served the odd shift as supervisor when the need arose and there was little animosity towards the owners. Katherine's preference was definitely for the bar. She felt more at home there. She didn't like people who had pretentions and the hotel, for all that it was a little run down, still aimed a little higher than the lowest common denominator in the products it was selling. Still, sometimes it became necessary for her to go to the hotel instead of the bar. Mainly when she was banned after an act of brutal violence.

The latest of her many fist-fights happened in 1972 when she was seventeen. One of the new miners who had arrived in town took an immediate dislike to David Kellett, despite his general popularity among the workers in the abattoir. Whilst the two pillars of industry within Aberdeen rarely brushed against one another, this bar was one of the few places where both sets of workers would meet. The miners typically drank in their own union-house, where the prices were better and membership was a requirement, but when they were feeling amorous, heading out into the general population was the only way they could hope to meet women. It is possible that the gentleman in question had taken a shine to Katherine, who was currently quite fixated on David, but the exact nature of their disagreement still isn't known. All that is certain is that when he insulted David Kellett to his face, the slaughterhouse worker backed down instead of escalating the situation. David wasn't a line worker like the rest of them—he drove one of the delivery trucks that served the abattoir—still, despite that degree of estrangement, he was well aware that his comrades from the meat-works would back him if it came to a fight. Ultimately, he just didn't want that sort of trouble in his life. David was a relatively calm man of twenty-two years. If questioned, he would simply say that he had nothing to prove to anyone—that he was out for a quiet drink, not a brawl. The truth was, David was not a particularly physically imposing man and, in a small community of miners and heavy manual labourers, he just couldn't stack up in terms of bulk or raw strength.

Katherine did not share his compunctions or his limitations. Since she had started her new career in the meat-works, her father's genetics had won out. Any hint of waifishness had vanished as her muscles filled out and a final growth spurt had left her towering over David at six foot tall.

When the insult had been flung, her face turned beetroot red: a visual warning that would follow her through her life each time that her rage consumed her. She swung for the miner and she didn't stop until her knuckles were bloody and his teeth were scattered over the bare floorboards. David had to drag her off before she could kill the man—with the assistance of a good number of her stronger co-workers.

It was passed off by the other men in the bar as high spirits, as a drunken brawl, something that could happen to anyone. But what only Katherine and the bartender knew for certain was that her glass held only lemonade. She drank with the rest of them, held her own drink by drink because she never touched alcohol. She had seen how it robbed men of their power and she had no intention of ever feeling powerless again. The bartender had never shared that secret, assuming that the woman was just trying to protect herself against the lustful, leering men all around her, but he still knew and it still informed his decision to ban her. There was no liquor to excuse her actions; they were all just Katherine being Katherine.

With no bar to attend, both Katherine and David were forced to relocate to the hotel for the next night and it was there that they finally got together. He had been amazed that she would stand up for him like that, that any woman would throw a punch to avenge an insult against a man. In all of his life, he'd never felt so wanted.

It soon became clear that devotion wasn't all that Katherine brought to the relationship. Instead of subsisting on whatever could be scrounged up at the meat-works mess hall, David was soon dining on elaborate home-cooked meals. His clothes were being mended and their sex life quickly became a thing of legend. Everyone suspected that there was a little bit of animal in Katherine, but her appetite astounded David. And, when he was in his cups and talking about her, they astounded everyone else

RYAN GREEN

in town, too. Just as her father had ravaged Barbara up to ten times a day, so was his daughter equally insatiable in her pursuit of sex—not so much for her own enjoyment, but to prove her absolute devotion, body and soul, to David.

For a man like him, this was overwhelming. He was used to living a hard life and all of this kindness turned his head. More than that, the change in Katherine stunned him. He had only known her as the quick-to-anger co-worker; he had never experienced the soft side of Katherine that used to be her primary personality. Whatever reservations he had harboured about a potential relationship faded away rapidly and before long, the two of them had moved in together.

Twenty years on from when Ken and Barbara had been run out of town for living in sin, attitudes had shifted a little. The fact that Katherine didn't give a damn about the opinion of anyone who might be muttering helped, as did the expectation that even though the two of them were dallying at the moment, they were definitely on course towards marriage. They had a brief period of equilibrium when they were living together 'in sin' and working together in perfect harmony, but then, external forces began intruding. Katherine's flirtatious way of speaking to co-workers who were in her favour riled up David's usually subdued temper and he was soon being needled by their wives—by proxy—to tie the knot and keep everything respectable. Like Katherine, he was something of an outsider to Aberdeen society, so the pressure didn't trouble him too much.

Unfortunately, Katherine soon had the idea planted in her head that, without the guarantee of marriage, David was likely to leave her, and that the reason he was refusing to commit to marriage was because that had been his intention all along: to have sex with her for as long as it suited him and then to abandon her and move on to the next town when she became too much of a burden. In the echo chamber of Katherine's mind, these ideas bounced back and forth until they were almost deafening. Eventually, she went from dropping hints to outright demanding

46

that David marry her. That, if he loved her, he would marry her. If he was faithful, he had to.

David had only been neglecting to marry Katherine because he thought that she had no interest. Now that her opinions had changed, he was happy to go along with her. He didn't think he'd ever meet a match like her again, so why on earth wouldn't he want to tie the knot?

There were certain formalities that had to be addressed before the wedding could move forward. Ones that both Katherine and David had been more than happy to avoid up until now. She took him out to meet her parents.

With decent savings filed away and his daughter still nipping at his heels, Ken had finally begun the slow slide into retirement. What was left of the Knight family had withdrawn from the meat-works' barracks—where their reputation had been in steady decline ever since their arrival—and relocated to a run-down farmhouse a little way out of Aberdeen town proper. Ken had cut back to only part-time shifts at the abattoir and was spending the rest of his time trying to get the house into some semblance of order. The vast majority of the land attached to the farm had been parcelled out to neighbours once the bank foreclosed on the previous tenants, transforming it from a source of income for the family into nothing more than an isolated dwelling in an advanced state of disrepair.

With his advancing age, Ken was finally starting to treat Barbara a little more gently, if only because he no longer had the energy to chase her around the house, batter her senseless and rape her ten times a day anymore. There was a stale quality to the air, where once tension had filled every living space. Ken and David had met before whilst working together, so whilst there was a little awkwardness regarding the fact that he was now dating Ken's daughter, they soon fell back into the usual comfortable companionable rhythm. Barbara was another story entirely. Much like Katherine, a decade without proper socialisation had left her a little rough around the edges. She'd always been prone to foul language—she was the font of knowledge from which most of Katherine's obscenities had been learned—but now it seemed to be almost all the vocabulary she had at her disposal. A brutally hard life had worn her down until she was little more than animal.

Eventually, Barbara cornered David in the heart of her domain, when he'd ducked into the kitchen to fetch Ken and himself another can of beer.

'You want to marry her, do you?'

He nodded, all the nervousness he'd carried into the house coming back to him in a rush now that it was being spoken about so bluntly.

'You sure about that? You know she's got a screw loose?'

David let out a startled laugh. He couldn't believe that Katherine's own mother was talking about her like that.

'I know she's got a little temper, yeah.'

Barbara tutted. 'Nah. You don't. Don't understand at all, do you?'

He shrugged and started backing away towards the kitchen door. Barbara was flushed, a few beers in herself and getting twitchy. 'You'd better watch that one or she'll fucking kill you. Stir her up the wrong way or do the wrong thing and you're fucked. Don't ever think of playing up on her, she'll fucking kill you.'

David chuckled. He'd been expecting this sort of warning from Ken, the old 'treat my girl right' threats that most fathers inflicted, but he'd never expected his future mother-in-law to be warning him about bad behaviour this way.

He smiled at Barbara. 'Don't you worry, I'll treat her well.'

'I'm not worried.' The woman was aged before her time, wrinkled and exhausted already. She stared out of the window and added, 'Ain't me she'll kill if it goes tits up.'

David didn't believe a word of it. He'd seen no hint of danger in Katherine, even when she drew knives on the men in the abattoir or beat a miner unconscious with her bare hands. To him, she was the perfect, charming wife that he had always hoped to secure for his future. He wasn't going to let anyone's wild suspicions ruin the best hope he had for his future.

With that settled and the arrangements made, the wedding day swiftly approached, pencilled into the calendar for just a few days after Katherine turned eighteen. There was no registry office in Aberdeen; the town was just too small to justify one. When the time for the subdued ceremony arrived, David had already been drinking heavily with his friends in the bar, both to provide him with some 'Dutch courage' and as a part of the celebrations. The indignant Katherine had to wait outside the bar in her handmade wedding dress until he came out, loaded her on the back of his motorbike and drove them, in a serpentine fashion, to the next town over.

The ceremony was the cheapest that money could buy, with the intention being to head back to the bar and spend the difference that they'd saved on a raucous party. Despite David's inebriation, he made it through the ceremony without incident and Katherine was so happy it seemed like she was going to let these minor slights slide. After they'd signed the license, they hopped back onto the bike and headed off down the dusty road back to Aberdeen.

The rest of the day was devoted to drinking, David's favourite hobby. In addition to all the usual suspects from the abattoir, his extended family was in attendance, along with as many of Katherine's relatives as could be convinced to make an appearance. The two groups did not mix. The Knights' reputation preceded them and whilst David's family were mostly visiting from Queensland, they had been forewarned by friends in the area about what they were likely walking into.

Over the course of the day, Katherine was insulted over and over by the Kellett family. They thought that she was too stupid to understand their little jibes, but whilst she lacked the communication skills required to make her intelligence apparent, there was a lethal cunning lurking just behind her

49

eyes, and she had lived as the school bully for long enough to know when insults were being flung around. She blocked them all out. This was the happiest day of her life and if some piece of shit out-of-towners couldn't be happy for her then what the hell did she care. It was her day. Her's and David's.

In a state of advanced inebriation, the two of them made their way back to David's company-issued apartment to consummate their new union. Katherine was always enthusiastic, but on their wedding night, she was practically ecstatic, tearing David's clothes off and rushing him through to the bedroom so fast that they forgot to lock the door behind them.

They had sex three times in quick succession, with Katherine coaxing David on past the limits of his usual endurance. After that third time, he passed out immediately and Katherine was suddenly left alone in the tempest of her own thoughts and passions. When he started snoring, her fury bubbled over. All of the frustration of the day—all of the tension that she had been bundling up inside her that she was so used to unleashing immediately by lashing out at the earliest provocation—it all came boiling over. She beat at David with her bare hands to wake him up, slapping him and punching him until it became apparent that he was too numbed by alcohol to recognise any of her abuse. Then, her incoherent rage turned lethal. She climbed on top of his unconscious body, wrapped her hands around his throat and started to squeeze the life out of him.

Some spark of self-preservation was still inside of his drunken husk. Before brain-damage could kick in, David awoke. He was confused more than he was angry. The alcohol, lack of blood to the brain and his sudden awakening all combined to create a kaleidoscope of chaos that he couldn't comprehend, much less deal with. He didn't try to defend himself once he'd wrestled himself free of her strangling grasp. Instead, he staggered out of the room, gasping for air.

Pain finally started to penetrate the haze. The scratches. The slaps. The bruises forming all over his skin. He couldn't explain it. He couldn't understand what had happened to him when the only memory that he had of the moments before were of blissful, carnal joy.

'Kathy, what the hell?'

He could barely see her in the dark shadows of their unlit apartment. Her bare skin would give him pale glimpses in the moonlight, warning him where she was and how swiftly she was approaching, but he couldn't see her face. He had no way of knowing which of the two Katherines he was trapped here with. Whether her face would be flushed red with her berserk fury, or if she'd faded back to her usual lovely self, the woman to whom he'd just sworn the rest of his life.

She lurched forward out of the darkness and pressed her lips to his, clumsily. 'Thought you'd fallen asleep on me there. Ready to go again?'

He wheezed out a pained breath that he hadn't realised he was holding. She was back to her normal self. Or as normal as Kathy got. David backed away from her and Kathy's hands flexed convulsively, like she wanted to grab onto him.

He groaned. 'You choked me?'

'What? Just a little.' She looked sheepish for a moment, like a little kid that had been caught doing something naughty, then in a snap, the fire was back in her voice. 'Don't be a pansy. You weren't waking up.'

She reached for him again and this time her fingers tangled in his chest hair before he could get out of reach. He growled, 'So you thought you'd just choke me, you mad bitch?'

'Don't you talk to your wife like that you ugly little bastard. You married me. That means you're mine.' She dragged him closer. 'So you get your lazy drunken arse back in that bedroom and fuck. You hear me?'

He took a hold of her wrists and managed to pry her free. 'You're nuts. You've got a screw loose. The old bag tried to warn me but I didn't listen.'

Katherine was lost in her own thoughts, too wound up to even understand what he was saying to her. 'Daddy did it five times. We've got to do it more.'

'What? What the hell are you talking about?'

Katherine's eyes were glazed over, lost in memory. 'On their wedding night, my Daddy did it with Barb five times. You love me, don't you? You love me more than that, right? We've got to fuck again. Two more times. At least two more. We've got to.'

He backed away from her, horrified. If the violence hadn't been enough to put him off any further amorous overtures—and there were plenty of men that it wouldn't have—then this talk about her parent's sex life, the explicit details that Barbara had poured out into her daughters, would have been enough to kill his passion. She blinked away her own confusion and gave him a coy smile, 'David. Don't worry about all that. It is just a little fight. Everybody has a little fight once they're married. Come on now. Come back to bed. I'll kiss it all better.'

He took a deep breath. He could still feel where her fingers had been biting into his throat. A deep, dull ache that didn't want to fade. A warning. Even the rush of adrenaline hadn't been able to drive all the day's drunkenness away, but some rational part of his mind was working now. Some basic survival instinct was picking up the slack.

'All right, love. You head to bed. I'll just ... nip to the loo and meet you there, yeah?'

She licked her lips. 'Don't be too long or I'll start without you.'

He managed to muster a smile before she skulked off. The bathroom was the only door in the house that had a lock and whilst he wouldn't be able to explain it in the cold light of day, he went into the bathroom, turned that lock and climbed into the bath to fall asleep. Katherine came hammering at the door not ten minutes later, but the booze-riddled sleep that had gotten him into so much trouble before turned into his salvation. Too drunk to waken, he couldn't get up to let the raging Katherine into the room.

Marital Bliss

After that initial hiccup, the marriage swiftly became bliss all over again. The two of them returned to their respective jobs, but whilst David slumped in from work, tired, all of the carnage that surrounded Katherine all day had her leaving the meat-works so full of energy she was practically bouncing. She washed all of David's clothes, cooked all of his meals, kept their communal living space absolutely pristine, and, when they were ready to move into a bigger place together, she handled all of the heavy lifting involved—both figurative and literal.

She was the perfect wife in every regard and within a week David had written off her marital night shenanigans as a misunderstanding that he had probably perpetuated in his drunken state. Like her teachers when she pulled a knife on another student, David was incapable of reconciling the two images that he had of Katherine, so he chose to believe in the one that benefited him the most. The beautiful young wife who willingly pandered to his every whim and who completely adored him.

This honeymoon period stretched out for weeks, then months. Katherine began to buckle under the strain of perfection, though. She was still able to let out her violent impulses in the odd workplace argument and the gruesome work that she did each day still gave her the same old satisfaction, but she was pushing herself every moment that she was with David to be the perfect wife and, eventually, something was going to have to give.

It did not escalate straight to another act of violence, but Katherine's temper began to manifest itself in other ways. She still performed every one of her many wifely duties without fail or complaint, but now she began to pick at any perceived faults in David. If he was home a minute later than he'd said he would be, she started to make wild accusations of infidelity. The pattern of a marriage was well established in her own mind and she saw none of the raw animal lust in David that had kept her parents together. Without that, she had to assume that their relationship would go exactly the same way as the first marriage that her mother had described to her in intimate detail. First, love, then marriage, then betrayal. To Katherine, the idea of David leaving her was so intensely painful, that just the thought of it began to poison their relationship.

The accusations persisted throughout the first year of their relationship when David was still working as a truck driver, out of her sight all day long. In a concession to her delusions, David took a job on the abattoir line at a fairly significant wage cut so that she could keep an eye on him all day long. He had assumed that if there were no possibility that he was being unfaithful, then her irrational behaviour would come to a halt and their happy relationship could resume. This was not the case.

By 1975, the constant accusations and foul treatment at the hands of Katherine were beginning to wear on David. It didn't matter anymore that her insane behaviour changed faster than the weather and that his beloved wife returned and did everything in her power to make things up to him; he was exhausted from living in a constant state of tension, just waiting for the next attack to come. On top of that, he was completely unsuited to his new job in the meat-works. Whilst his slight build had been a perfect fit in the cab of a lorry, on the abattoir floor he was dwarfed by the other men and he had to push himself to the limits of his strength just to keep up with the rest of the line. He began to go out drinking with his co-workers more and more often. Katherine's accusations came less frequently when they were in public and her other foul treatment at least had the benefit of earning him some sympathy from the other married men. Before long, the constant outings to the bar started to cut into the time that Katherine used for housekeeping and standards began to slip in their home. She was forced with the choice to either continue dogging David's steps to ensure that he was faithful to her or returning to the old routine in which she felt like she was being a good wife, one that was worthy of affection and devotion.

That particular internal struggle stretched on for many months, with Katherine flip-flopping back and forth between the two options, running herself ragged trying to do both, spending one night at home playing catch up and the next out with David, pretending that everything was fine. Desperately pretending that everything in their marriage was fine when she could feel him pulling away from her more and more every day.

One night, when the two of them were visiting Ken and Barbara for an awkward attempt at family bonding, Katherine came to an epiphany. Her father had his flaws, but he had never cheated on her mother and that had to be for a reason. Katherine still held that infidelity was a fundamental part of a man's makeup, but even the most broken and twisted relationship that she had ever encountered in her life had managed to resist it. She had to assume that it was because Barbara did everything that she was meant to do.

From that day forward, Katherine let David run free. She stayed home after work, put a beautiful home-cooked meal on the table every night and tended to his every whim when he finally elected to come home. She still fell into her rages, still made her wild accusations, but those were things that she considered to be outside of her control. Taking care of him properly was something that she could do.

A new equilibrium was established, one that probably could have been maintained forever if nothing else changed. David was willing to put up with her insane rambling, even managing to convince himself that it was just her way of showing that she loved him, because of the royal treatment that he received the rest of the time.

In August, she fell pregnant and her jealousy and obsession with David jumped into overdrive. The idea of being abandoned had terrified her before, but the idea of being abandoned whilst pregnant pushed the catastrophic scenarios that she was imagining to a whole new level. She was hyper-aware of absolutely everything that David said and did. Just a word out of place could set her off screaming and cursing him. One day, after a long shift at the meat-works, David came home to change into a clean shirt before heading to the bar. This was not his usual routine and Katherine latched onto it immediately.

Who was he getting dressed up for? Who was he sneaking off to meet in his fancy new shirt? The shirt she had sewn for him. The unbelievable bastard. All these months he had been lying to her, claiming that he loved her. Pretending that he cared about her. Now he'd knocked her up and he was off chasing after some other girl. Well, they would just see about that. Let's see how handsome she thinks he is when he doesn't have any new clothes to go dancing around in. Let's see how much of a hit he is with the ladies with just the shirt on his back.

She gathered up all of his other clothes in the bathtub, doused them in lighter fluid and tossed in a match. The ensuing blaze brought the haphazardly-assembled Aberdeen fire department to their door and, since half of those men were dragged out of the bar to come and throw a few buckets of water into the Kellett family bathroom, David came along for the ride, too.

The bathroom roof had turned black with soot, smoke had flooded out through the rest of the house, choking Katherine until she'd run outside. It was painfully apparent what had happened inside the house—the evidence was melted into the bathtub, after all. The whole world was now witness to Katherine and David's dysfunctional relationship and, whilst he burned with shame, she just turned her flushed face towards the whole town of Aberdeen and stared them down. Daring them to say a word.

Following the fire, David was too embarrassed to show his face in the bar for weeks. The two of them quietly relocated to a small house near to the abattoir when the cleaning required to make his apartment liveable again proved too extensive. He might have expected Katherine to be blissful now that she had him entirely to herself, but nothing could be further from the truth. She still accused him of infidelity on an almost hourly basis, like the slow machinery of her mind had developed a fault and kept clicking back into the same groove after it had been running unattended for too long. Their married life remained a constant alternating mixture of heaven and hell for David and, before long, he took to the bar again just to escape the onslaught.

One night, he returned home at about the same time that he usually staggered home for his dinner and Katherine ambushed him in their living room, screaming about him abandoning her, that he was off chasing after some other woman all over again. Burning his clothes hadn't been enough to fend all the loose women of Aberdeen off from him, so she decided something else needed burning. When he came home, she had been ironing what little wardrobe David had been able to piece together. With a roar, she swung the scalding hot iron at his face. It burned a thick gash across his cheek, searing through almost to his cheekbone. If he hadn't flinched away at exactly the right moment, the blow would have cost him his eye. He retreated, screaming in pain, to the bathroom—his old sanctuary from her violent outbursts—and locked the door before she could get to him. She hammered at the door with the iron, leaving burn marks and dents in equal measure until the rage left her just as suddenly as it had come on and she started weeping and begging forgiveness, whispering under the door that she was sorry, that she would never do it again, that she just missed him so much that it made her crazy. Despite the pain and disfigurement he had just suffered, David believed her. He unlocked the bathroom door and the two of them embraced. She wrapped his face in gauze and lavished kisses on his unmarked cheek. Before long, they moved into the bedroom, where she did her best to distract him from the pain.

David didn't sleep all night. Not because of Katherine's amorous attentions, although they were plentiful, but because of the awful pain in his face. He knew that if he called an ambulance then the paramedics would be obliged to report his injuries to the police and he didn't want to see Kathy get in trouble over something that had happened in a moment of passion. He lay there in the dark, with his wife snoring beside him and held back his screams.

The next day at work, David's supervisor took one look at the injury and drove him to the hospital to have it seen to. Without the emergency call, the police were not informed about what had happened. David got the help that he needed and Katherine got to avoid repercussions. It was the best of both worlds and all that it had cost was David lying in agony for eight hours instead of seeking medical attention for the grizzly burn scar that would remain his most prominent feature for the rest of his life.

In the aftermath of that assault, David began to make some new concessions to Katherine to help keep the peace. When she felt like he was running late, she would become upset with him, so he formalised his evening arrangements to prevent any more 'misunderstandings.'

Before they went their separate ways after work, he would list off his plans for the evening and she would either approve them or demand alterations. In her continuing quest to appear the perfect wife, she tried to let David feel like he was making the decisions, but she lacked the communication skills necessary to manipulate him with any sort of subtlety, so, more often than not, she would end up barking, 'No!' at him over and over until he accommodated her poorly-expressed demands.

He learned the hard way that this method of managing Katherine had its setbacks. One night, he lingered slightly too long at the bar before heading back towards the slaughterhouse and their company-provided home on 'Honeymoon Lane.' He was so close to being on time that it didn't even occur to him that Katherine might have a problem with it.

When he was one minute late, Katherine began to get anxious. She started to imagine that he had run off with someone else, that his long-awaited betrayal was finally here. She was now six months pregnant. The slaughterhouse kept dropping less and less subtle hints that she needed to stop working the line. She was going to be alone and unemployed with a baby. A baby that she didn't even know that she wanted.

When he was two minutes late, her catastrophic vision of the future faltered in the face of her blinding rage. He'd better not come home after making her wait this long. If he came home, she was going to slice him to pieces. She was going to make him pay for betraying her, running off with his women and abandoning his wife to suffer in silence, all alone.

When he was three minutes late, the capacity for rational thought had entirely escaped Katherine. Her mind was still rattling through elaborate plans for bloody revenge, but it was more like a series of flashing images shuddering past her mind's eye than any sort of coherent pattern.

He arrived back at the house four minutes after he was due to return. The lights had been turned out and it was completely silent. David let out a little huff of relief. Even if he didn't think Kathy was going to mind him coming in so close to her crazy curfew, he still didn't really want to deal with her right now. If she'd made him dinner and sulked off to bed early, like she did every now and again, then he was in for a nice, relaxing evening, followed by some of the vigorous lovemaking that Kathy always went in for when she was well-rested and feeling guilty about neglecting him. The night was looking up already.

Keeping it nice and quiet, he pulled open the door to the kitchen and stepped inside with a smile on his face.

He blinked once or twice. He was looking up at the stars. Why was he looking up at the stars? His stomach lurched. Where was he? The last thing that he remembered, he had been walking home. He had been at the bar. Maybe he was drunk? Maybe he'd fallen somewhere and hit his head. It felt kind of sore, but that pain was far away in the distance like it was on its way but hadn't quite arrived yet. He fluttered his eyes open and shut a few more times. Home. He had to get home. If he was late, Kathy would be furious.

He tried to sit up. That was when the pain caught up to him.

The bones in his head felt like they were grinding together. Like his whole skull was grinding and shrieking. The pain was intense, immediate and all-consuming. A blinding light in the darkness of the night. The only reason that he didn't scream was that his throat was clogged up with the wave of vomit that trying to move had conjured up out of him. It was splattered all over him now; his face was slick with it down one side. His mouth was sour with stale beer and bile. The pain wasn't distant now. Without movement, the grating had stopped but it still felt like molten metal was trapped inside his head.

Something had happened.

What had happened? It was almost impossible to work it out with the pain dragging him back every time he tried to think, every time he tried to remember. When he tried to move, the pain got worse, he wanted to die every time he moved. He let out a little whimper, but even that slight vibration set his skull thrumming all over again. There was an echo of that sound that dragged his memory back into the light. A noise like a gong being sounded.

The cast-iron frying pan swung at the back of his head with all of the brutal force that the powerful arms of Katherine could muster.

David let out a whimper and raised a nervous hand up to touch the wetness on the back of his head. He half expected to find it caved in and it was almost a relief when his fingertips touched blood-soaked hair. Almost a relief, because the moment that he applied any pressure, he could feel his skull shifting beneath his skin. The pain rose like the sun, blinding him to everything else.

It took him an hour to drag himself inch by painful inch to the back door of the neighbouring house. Twenty minutes more to muster the strength to scrape and bang loud enough to draw some attention. By then, he was completely incoherent. His neighbours, the Macbeths, couldn't do anything but call an ambulance as he sunk back down into nightmare-haunted unconsciousness.

David awoke the next day, just ten miles from where he'd fallen, in Muswellbrook Hospital, with his wife simpering by his bedside, holding his hand, with tears in her eyes.

A number of scenarios could explain what he chose to do next.

It is possible that he was taken in by Katherine's 'perfect wife' act the way that he had been so many times in the past. Despite everything that had happened, David was deeply in love with Katherine, or at least his idealised version of her. He may have thought that this would be a turning point in their relationship, a pivot back on to the right course. Guilt over one irrational act had been sufficient to reshape many people into better versions of themselves—it wasn't entirely wishful thinking that the harmless-looking, sobbing pregnant woman at his bedside would be one of them.

It is equally possible that he was frightened to think what Katherine would do to him if he spoke out against her. They were in a hospital, he was weak and helpless and she still had every bit of the terrible strength that she had unleashed against him the previous night.

One final factor was the testosterone-drenched culture of rural Australia in the 70s. A place where men were meant to be tough and women subservient. It would have been a dreadful blow to David's ego and his reputation in the community if it became known that he was being beaten by his wife. The shame of everyone knowing how Katherine had burnt his clothes had been enough to drive him into hermitage before, and that was widely-excused as a common act of hysterical womanhood that could be mocked and made light of. This was something much more serious, something that could strip him of his manhood entirely if he let it.

When the police arrived to take the couple's report of what had happened the night before, David explained it away. Katherine had been left home alone when he went out drinking and when she heard someone trying to get into the house she acted in self-defence. An accident, rather than an act of malevolent brutality. It was an easy-to-swallow story for the New South Wales Police, who preferred not to get involved in domestic violence cases when the man was the perpetrator in those days, let alone this strange, flipped version. Katherine was happy to reiterate his story to them from her perspective, being sure to look at him pointedly every time she repeated how late her husband had been in returning home.

With the concussion and subsequent damage to his brain, it is possible that David genuinely couldn't recall the events of the previous night properly and he was forced to accept that Katherine's version of events was genuine due to having no alternative explanation to hand. After all, it wasn't like she had explained why she was assaulting him before swinging at him with the skillet. She had been too lost in her fury to even formulate words, let alone sentences. Her limited vocabulary was a hindrance at the best of times, but in moments of duress, she became almost entirely mute, letting out little more than snarls and growls like some sort of wild animal trapped in a human body.

A few days later, when the swelling around his brain had eased and the doctors were convinced that the fragmented sections of his skull were beginning to knit back together, David was released into Katherine's custody and she took him home. He was guided to their bed with her arms hooked under his, laid out carefully on a heap of pillows and kissed gently on the cheek. If he had been hoping for a change in Katherine, then this was surely it. The perfect wife had returned. She pampered him for the rest of the week, tending to his every need and desire with the same brazen admiration she had shown him when they were courting. David truly came to believe that his nightmare was finally over.

When David returned to work, Katherine finally gave in to the boss' prodding and stayed home, after getting assurances that her job would still be waiting for her when she returned from her unofficial maternity leave. Alone in the house all day, it didn't take long for Katherine's imagination to start running away from her all over again. Worse yet, David seemed to have lost all fear of crossing her. Now that she was showing him nothing but sweetness, he had forgotten who he was dealing with.

It didn't take long before she reminded him.

One night, less than a month after the first near-lethal assault, her veneer of benevolence started to chip away. She had been taking long drives in the countryside during her empty days, swerving to hit cats and dogs when she saw them. It was the only amusement that she could come up with for herself that didn't involve any strenuous physical activity or company. David had dinner with her after he'd finished work, then immediately got up to leave for a darts tournament at the bar. He checked that Katherine was all right with this plan and took her smiling agreement at face value, but before he left, she made sure to confirm what time the tournament would be over. Once she knew it was 11 pm, she settled in for another night of quiet crafting, working on new clothes for David and the baby.

When 11 pm arrived and David hadn't, she didn't immediately fly into a rage. She had been working on her temper as a part of her plans to keep David sweet, so instead of letting herself descend into the usual downward spiral of imagined slights, she phoned the bar and asked to speak with him.

'I thought you were coming home?'

He actually had the courage to sound annoyed with her. 'I am, I am. The tourney is just running a bit long, is all. Shouldn't be more than an hour.'

'But you said you'd be back at eleven.'

David was in front of all of his friends from the meat-works—if he went skulking off at Katherine's beck and call, he would never live it down. 'Well, now I'm saying I won't.'

She was waiting for him when he got home. Frying pan in hand. This time he was ready for her. He ducked out of the way of her first swing, caught the second one on his arm instead of his face. Katherine had turned completely red. She was huffing instead of breathing. She looked like some sort of mythical monster more than she looked like a woman. The next swing missed him entirely and knocked a light switch off the wall instead.

In the darkness and screaming chaos that ensued, David managed to get out of the house, running back down the road towards the bar and catching up to his drinking buddies before they could all disperse. He spent the night on one of their sofas, delaying the inevitable retribution until the next day.

He went to work as usual and fully expected Katherine to show up there to claim him, but instead, he just had a whole day of back-breaking labour with the constant threat of violence hanging over him. People in prison were living better than him.

For all that he was in love with Katherine and overflowing with forgiveness, David Kellet finally came to a conclusion whilst he was scraping marrow out of bones that day. If he didn't get away from her, she was going to kill him.

The idea had been percolating in his head for quite some time, but the attack the night before had just cemented his certainty, in no small part because Katherine's suspicions about him were actually correct.

Ever since Katherine had first started wildly accusing him of infidelity, David had been alienated and isolated in his marriage, so he had done the only thing that made sense to him. He'd gone looking for affection elsewhere. It hadn't been an active search, but it had been a fruitful one and, shortly before Katherine seared her mark into his face, he had formed an ongoing relationship with a girl whom he knew in Queensland. After his concussion, he had stepped up his plans to be with her and just a week before she had informed him that she, too, was pregnant with his child. She wanted him to leave Katherine and for them to be a family. The whistle of the frying pan being swung at his head the night before was like the sounding of a starter pistol. He needed to escape; he had somewhere to escape to. Now all that he needed was the opportunity to get out alive.

He returned home that night to find that Katherine had transformed back into her loving and devoted personality. He apologised profusely for being late the night before, explained that he completely understood why she was angry and did everything in his power to make it up to her, even bringing her flowers and some freshly-cut pork chops for dinner. She was so smitten with the gesture that all of his sins were forgotten.

He spent the next month and a half walking on eggshells, just waiting for the opportunity to grab his things and get the hell out of town, but the chance wouldn't arrive until May of 1976 when Katherine went into labour.

Katherine's parents were called and they rushed over to drive her to Muswellbrook Hospital, leaving David behind to pack a bag for her and follow after. He packed all of his surviving belongings into that bag, walked down to the slaughterhouse and handed in his notice. With a spring in his step, he got into his car and drove out of Aberdeen as fast as he could, before anyone could report back to the Knight family. He was free, at last.

Alone in the Dark

Katherine went through a long and painful labour to bring her first daughter, Melissa Ann, into the world, and she spent almost every moment of it asking for her husband. Sobbing. Screaming his name with each contraction all through the long night. Her sister was sent off from the hospital to scour Aberdeen for any sign of him. He had left the vast majority of his belongings behind—whether out of guilt or simply a desire to travel light and get away fast—which obscured the fact that he was truly missing. His car was gone, as was the case that he was meant to have packed for Katherine, so the abiding assumption was that something had happened to him on the road to the hospital. Joy swiftly recruited some of his friends from the meat-works' barracks to search for him and it wasn't long before a half dozen cars were flying about the back-roads around Aberdeen in search of a crashed car.

Joy was a little more suspicious than David's friends, however. She had grown up in the same household as Katherine, hearing the same gruesome and lewd stories about the qualities of men from their mother. She knew the evil that lurked in their hearts and, whilst Katherine had found a way to master it, Joy still lived in fear of it. None of the men in his usual haunts had seen David. None of the neighbours wanted to get involved in another of Katherine's screaming rages, which were gradually becoming legendary about town, so they were all struck blind to his movements, too. It was only when dawn rolled around that it occurred to Joy that there might have been some sort of work emergency that dragged him away from the birth of his first child. She went to the abattoir to ask after him and discovered that he'd quit.

By the time that Katherine had given birth and was capable of independent thought and movement again, she had sunk into a deep rage. Despite her blood loss during labour, that familiar red flush filled her face. Those that were unfortunate enough to know her recognised these signs and retreated with as much tact as they could muster, but the hospital staff didn't get much more than grunts and growls from her when they delivered the baby into her arms for feeding, or when they plucked Melissa off her breast when the tiny baby had drunk her fill.

Whatever love she might have felt for her daughter at that moment, whatever bond a normal mother would make with the tiny life that she had just brought into the world, was washed away by Katherine's black mood. Her eyes darted to the door of the ward every time there was movement, but David still had not arrived. At the moment when she was most vulnerable—when she needed her husband by her side the most—he had abandoned her. Her vengeance was going to be a gruesome thing, a bloody nightmare, the likes of which Aberdeen had never seen. She was going to do things to David that would have made the old man who tortured pigs for laughs sick to his stomach. She had her knives hanging above her bed at home and by god was she going to use them. That worthless scumbag would never walk again. Let's see how far away from her he got when he couldn't even walk, when she snipped every tendon in his legs and left him limp as the worthless, wailing little lump in her arms. He would never leave her again—she'd keep him like one of the broken-winged birds she used to hoard in her bedroom, powerless and desperate for every bit of attention she gave him—just as soon as she got her hands on him.

Joy had always been in her sister's blind spot, never a victim of her cruelty, nor an authority figure who needed to be appeased or navigated. She may very well have been the only person in the world whom Katherine actually considered to be a friend. Out of all the people in her life, only Joy could deliver the news of David's escape safely, without fear of violent repercussions.

She expected Katherine to rage and scream—to lose her mind to the fury that still clearly consumed her—but instead, she had to sit and watch her sister break. The red flush faded from her face, the knotted muscles of her jaw went slack and her eyes went dead. She was too devastated to even cry. She whispered a soft, 'Thank you,' then rolled away onto her side.

Normally, a mother was released from the hospital a few days after the baby was born, but both Katherine and Melissa Ann seemed to be sick. They lay lifeless and limp in a bed together. The only sounds being the occasional shriek of the baby as it demanded something. Katherine did not speak to her daughter. She barely even looked at her. Psychiatry was still in relative infancy at this point in history, isolated in specialist hospitals away from all of the 'normal' patients. So, there was an assumption that Katherine's illness was due to some complication of the birth, that her lifelessness and muteness were due to a lack of blood, or some damage to a nerve.

Eventually, the doctors were forced to give up and release her. Her father drove her home to the abandoned house. Neither father nor daughter had a word to say to the other the whole trip. Ken delivered the pram, which the Knights had bought the baby as a gift, to the doorstep right alongside his daughter, then turned and left without another word. What was there to say?

That first night, Katherine went through all the motions of being a good mother, just like she had always wanted when she was growing up. But, just like her own mother, it wasn't long before she started to pour her misery out onto the baby, too.

Regaling the child with endless stories about David's imagined infidelities, shortcomings as a man both in and out of the bedroom and, more generally, about how wicked he was to abandon the two of them. Whatever answer she was hoping to get from the baby did not seem to be forthcoming.

It took only a few weeks of being trapped alone in the house with Melissa before the darkest parts of Katherine's psyche took the helm. She'd always had limited patience with being stuck indoors and the addition of the constant shrill screaming of a baby pushed her past that limit in moments. Each morning, Katherine would rise with the sun, the same way that she always had, then she would load the baby into her pram and start walking up and down the streets of Aberdeen, desperate for some distraction from the misery of her life. People could not look her in the eye. At the best of times, an abandoned mother would have been a shameful sight, someone to be pitied as well as treated with contempt; but, in the case of Katherine Knight—the hellion of Honeymoon Lane—that pity never managed to come to fruition. There was too much fear of Katherine for anyone to reach out to her. Everyone knew that it was just a matter of time before she violently exploded in exactly the same way that she always had before and nobody wanted to be in the blast radius when it finally happened.

Her isolation was complete. Whether she was trapped in the house or roaming the streets, Katherine moved in a bubble of silence, pierced only rarely by the screams of Melissa. It did not take long for Katherine, sunken into a deep and dark depression, to loathe that sound. To long for the silence and isolation that had until now haunted her. She would never be able to pinpoint the exact moment that she started to hate her baby, but it is possible that Melissa served as a reminder of David's betrayal each time that Katherine looked at her. The thing that should have been her greatest joy, her greatest triumph in her pursuit of traditional conservative womanhood, had instead become a lead weight around her neck. A symbol of all the ways that her life had gone wrong.

By the end of May, Katherine was past her breaking point and diving headlong into cartoonish villainy. People twitched back their curtains to watch her as she went by, screaming and raving at the three-week-old baby in her pram. She took off, running down the streets, paying no heed to the way that the baby was flung around as she went over the potholes and bumps. When even that wasn't enough to calm Melissa, she started flinging the pram from side to side as she ran, battering the helpless baby off the hard sides of the pram as she mock-screamed right back into the tiny girl's face.

The Aberdeen police had learned to fear the wrath of Katherine Knight, even if they hadn't been on the receiving end of it themselves and had only seen the mess that she left of the people she raised her fists to. When they received a call about her that morning, they were far from surprised—it had always just been a matter of time before they were forced to face off with her. In such a small town, rumours ran rampant and a decent police force knew exactly how to turn that to its advantage. Community policing may be a buzzword of modern law enforcement, but in a town like Aberdeen, it was unavoidable and essential. The police lived in the same communities that they were policing and they heard the same whispers as anyone else—whether directly or through their wives—and that informed the way that they pursued their cases. The Katherine Knight that they knew was only one unlucky day away from a murder charge. They'd heard all about her treatment of David Kellet and, whilst they shared the same assumptions as everyone else at the time about her acts of domestic violence being retaliatory rather than predatory, they were also aware of just how easily self-defence could turn bloody—particularly out here, so far from the centres of civilisation.

Three officers were sent out to confront Katherine after her reckless endangerment of the baby had been called in, but the sight that confronted them was not what they had prepared for. Instead of the raging monster of bar-room legend, they were confronted by a helpless woman in tears. She started to sob as soon as they approached her, her face completely flushed and her voice quavering with every word she tried to bark out. Once again, when confronted with authority challenging her for her crimes, she managed to make them all someone else's fault.

Whilst they believed her fragmented story of abandonment and betrayal, the police still couldn't let her go roaming free, not when there was a child at risk. They offered her a ride home, offered to take the baby to her parents for the night and then drove her to the nearest hospital equipped to deal with mental health patients before she could realise what was happening around her.

St Elmo's Hospital in Tamworth was quiet about its area of specialisation, so as not to spook the local population. Everyone agreed that there should be hospitals for the insane, but nobody wanted one in their own back yard. The odd rumour might occasionally spread about the place, but if it did, it had never reached as far as Katherine's ears all the way out in Aberdeen. She had no idea why she was being taken to the hospital, loudly insisting at every turn that she wasn't sick, until eventually one of the nurses sat her down and explained exactly why she had been taken into their care. It was during this first stay in the hospital that the groundwork for much of the psychiatric casework about Katherine Knight was built.

There were strong suspicions, created from their gathered reports about her behaviour and her own strange admissions, that she suffered from BPD, but in the short term, all that they could prove conclusively was that she was suffering from a bout of post-natal depression, a mental condition that often presents in a failure to bond with the baby and, in extreme cases, results in attempts on the baby's life. Additional testing after that first day showed that Katherine had lost the ability to read and write since falling out of practice following her grand exit from the education system, and this, in turn, prompted the doctors to administer an IQ test, on which Katherine scored in the low 80s.

Even at this early stage in her diagnosis, the doctors began to suspect that the results that they were getting were not accurate. Whilst she lacked the education required to pass an IQ test, she did not lack in raw animal cunning. Coupled with the violent outbursts that she exhibited whenever she felt wronged, this drove one of the psychologists to describe her as being possessed of a 'primeval intelligence.' She operated on a very base level, akin to what you might expect from a caveman, rather than a woman in contemporary society. He was one of a few medical professionals who felt Katherine's mental health problems could more easily be explained away with a different diagnosis— psychopathy compounded with narcissism.

This tiny cabal within the hospital believed that Katherine was deliberately manipulating the other staff members so that she would be absolved of responsibility for her actions.

Throughout Katherine's life, she had a set pattern that she worked through if she was ever confronted by someone in a position of authority about her atrocities. At first, she would deny that her actions ever took place, as she had often done with her schoolyard bullying, violent threats towards her molesting brothers and vicious words towards others in the workplace. When that failed, due to evidence or testimony, she would instantly switch to admitting that the event had taken place, but it was at the behest of some other party for whom she was now taking the blame. This happened frequently during her week in St Elmo's, when she would fling accusations at other patients. Finally, when all else failed or there was no patsy to pin her crimes on, Katherine would admit to having committed them but insist that it was out of retribution for some slight against her— that her actions were a reasonable response to provocation from the party she had maimed or abused. With a formal diagnosis of BPD, Katherine would have had the ultimate freedom from responsibility for her actions. Her crimes would no longer be hers at all, even when there was nobody else to blame—they would be because of the BPD.

For this reason, among others, this minority of Katherine's carers intervened to ensure that her insanity defence was only temporary. Post-natal depression is an appalling, crippling mental illness, but it generally has a short run—even when it goes untreated. Katherine would be free to go after a short week in the institution, having undergone talk therapy—that she mainly responded to with grunts—and the beginnings of drug therapy that would go on for the rest of her life. With a paper bag full of pills and a clean bill of health, Katherine was released from St Elmo's less than seven days after her first attempt on Melissa's life.

She collected the baby from her parents in sullen silence, then went back home to the empty house that she had planned to share with her devoted husband for the rest of her days.

There was no sound from Katherine's house throughout the next day. The constant tirades of screaming that had accompanied every noise that the baby had made previously had given away to a more eerie silence. It was like the calm before the storm. Every time there was a sound, the neighbours would cast a fearful eye out of their windows, just waiting to see what new madness Katherine Knight might achieve, but nothing manifested, and by sunset many of them were starting to suspect that perhaps Katherine's stay in a mental hospital might actually have cured her, that the chaos and viciousness that they'd all been living with for years might finally have been brought low leaving nothing more than a lonely woman. Their hopes were misplaced.

'Old Ted' had worked in the mines for many years before an injury drove him out and now he lived a vagrant life, panhandling, foraging and receiving donations from the businesses around town to keep him fed and clothed. Despite his eccentricity and rather lax hygiene standards, he was fairly well-liked in Aberdeen, considered by many locals to be something of a local landmark. He had never run afoul of Katherine in his years of roaming about town. Not because he was beneath her notice—Katherine was strangely egalitarian with her viciousness, lashing out at all layers of society equally—but rather because he seemed to possess that same animal cunning that she did. Whatever else you could say about Old Ted, he was a survivor. And, he had lived as long as he had by recognising danger before it turned its attention on to him.

Whilst it would have been very easy for Ted to stay in the loop about all of the town's gossip, he wasn't inclined to seek it out and, more pressingly, he had spent most of the day since Katherine's release out of town, searching for game to hunt or crops that nobody would notice had gone missing. He knew nothing about the drama surrounding her, or the silence following her release.

So, as he trailed along the side of the train tracks in the cool evening, searching for the little brown mushrooms that sometimes grew between the wooden sleepers, oblivious to anything that might have been awry in town, he didn't think much of it when he heard a baby crying from up ahead. People about town left him alone, so he did his best to return the favour. If someone wanted to hold a crying baby by the train tracks, he wasn't going to stop them. Live and let live, that was his philosophy. But even his happy-go-lucky attitude began to get a little dented as the baby's wailing went on and on. He didn't have kids of his own, so he didn't have the experience to know the difference between a baby's cries, but this one was grating on him. It wasn't like it wanted something. It sounded pained or scared. He wished that its mother would just settle it down, just so he didn't have to hear it anymore. Not that he'd ever be so crude as to voice that opinion. He wasn't an animal.

The baby went on wailing and he went on tramping along the side of the tracks, doing his best to ignore it. There were a few mushrooms growing about here, so Ted crept a little closer to the tracks to pick them. That was when he felt the vibration running along the metal. A train was on its way and if he had any sense, he'd stand well clear. Most of them didn't stop in Aberdeen—they blew right through and, at that speed, they could lift a man right off his feet with the turbulence of their passing. Still, that baby went on crying up ahead. Ted finally felt like he should say something. The folks dithering by the line might not have known that a train was coming. He left the last of the mushrooms and jogged along the line, looking around but seeing no sign of anyone standing. He was almost standing on the baby before he realised what he was looking at.

Little Melissa was laid down on the tracks. Her head rattling on the rail as the train approached. With a yelp, Old Ted scooped her up, fumbling her as he tried to settle the wriggling lump safely in his arms. There was no time—he held Melissa out in front of him like a struggling cat and ran. The train ripped by a moment later, close enough on his heels that he felt it tugging on his coat-tails.

If he'd taken just a moment longer, the train would have run right over the baby, with nobody on board any the wiser.

Katherine had not been idle since abandoning her baby on the train tracks. She had walked back down into town in a fury, the likes of which Aberdeen had never even seen. Her face was flushed completely red, her brows drawn down so low that her eyes were lost in dark shadows. She seemed to have lost all ability to speak, huffing breaths in and out with a growl in her throat. She made a beeline for the general goods store in the middle of town, snatching up a wood-axe from the display and storming out into the street with a guttural roar.

The police were already on the scene by that point, having received a slew of informal warnings that Knight was on the move. She walked for a short distance down the road, swinging the axe back and forth in a figure of eight, but it didn't elicit the response she was looking for from the cowering onlookers. They might have feared her, but she could still see that disgusting pity in their eyes. They felt sorry for her. Mad little Katherine, abandoned by her cheating husband with a baby in tow. They wouldn't dare look at her like that again, not after what she had done tonight. That mewling little bitch Melissa was gone and Katherine was going to wipe Aberdeen off the map. Every one of these people was going to die until there was nobody left that could remember what had happened to her. She'd kill all of them, then she'd kill David, then she'd just go away somewhere and start over. It would be easy. She would be free again.

The police didn't dare come close to her. She was taller than any one of the officers sent out to fetch her and, with that axe in hand, she had enough of a reach to take a lump out of any one of them if they tried to come at her with billy-clubs. They trailed along, just out of reach, keeping everyone else out of her way as she stalked back and forth, swinging the axe around and around, growling and spitting and snarling, working herself up enough to make her charge.

She was almost ready to do it. She had almost built herself up enough that she really thought that she could kill them all. That was when the piercing wail cut through the tense silence of the standoff. Old Ted had come staggering down into town with a baby in his hands. The axe tumbled from Katherine's grip and the police rushed in to seize her. She let out an awful matching wail as she saw Melissa alive in the old man's arms, then she was buried under a pile of police trying to subdue her.

Her return to St Elmo's was brief. She was well-rehearsed in the correct things to say to be given a clean bill of health now and the staff were ready to admit that the dosage of her medication clearly hadn't been enough, calculated for the average woman rather than a lady of Katherine's bulk. Once she had been forcefully medicated, all traces of the raging berserker that had stalked the streets of Aberdeen were washed away once more. She was back to the charming, dim-witted girl whom they'd released only a day before. She signed herself out after spending a night in the hospital, then called her parents to come and collect her.

Ken and Barbara may not have been geniuses, but they recognised the pattern that was emerging and, for all of the personal evils that dominated their actions, they still couldn't bear the thought of their granddaughter being hurt, or worse. Ken drove Katherine home, but Melissa was not returned to her this time. He promised that the baby would be taken care of until Katherine was well again and no amount of threats or pleading were enough to change his mind.

Katherine was left completely and utterly alone.

The same dreadful silence descended over her house, but this time not even the cries of the baby punctured it. The neighbours kept watch on Katherine, both out of concern for a fellow human being and as an early warning system in case her murderous wrath was next directed towards them, but, yet again, there was nothing to see from dawn till dusk. This went on for three days. Three days of watching and waiting.

The Macbeths had always been relatively sympathetic to Katherine despite living right alongside her and hearing the worst of her screaming. They had been the family to help David receive medical treatment after his head injury and perhaps it was with that in mind that Katherine went to them on the night of the third day after her release.

Hearing a banging on the back door, 16-year-old Margaret Macbeth rushed to answer it, thinking that there was an emergency. Katherine was out there in tears. 'My baby is sick and I don't have my car. I need to get to her. Will you take me? Please?'

All of the foreboding stories that Maggie's parents had been sharing about Katherine went out the window the moment she saw those tears and heard those words. 'Of course. Let me grab the keys and my brother.'

'Your brother?' Katherine paused, lurking in the doorway.

'I'm babysitting him tonight. Don't worry. He'll come along with no trouble. Just head out to the car, I'll be with you in a second.'

Katherine was already in the passenger's seat by the time Maggie got shoes on her brother and shoved him out the door. They climbed into the car and were already in motion before Maggie asked, 'Where is your baby? At your parents'?'

'Queensland. We're going to Queensland.'

'What? That's a thousand miles away. What's your baby doing there?'

'Who gives a fuck about the baby? We're going to get David. His mum lives in Queensland. He'll be back on her apron strings. Him and his whore. They'll both be there with her. I'll see to them all.'

Maggie shivered and darted a glance over at Katherine. There was a butcher's knife resting in her lap. The dull yellow streetlights glinting off it as they passed under them. 'Kathy, I'm not sure I can drive you to Queensland. Is there somebody else who could ... '

Katherine growled, 'Shut up and drive.'

'I've got my little brother in the back. He's got school in the morning. I can't ... '

The knife was like an extension of Katherine's hand. For all that she stomped about town and clattered around in her house, there was a fluid grace to her movements now that she had a blade. It flicked out, almost of its own accord. Katherine didn't even have to look. It tore a line across Maggie's cheek. Deep enough that she could taste blood on the other side. Despite herself, Maggie screamed. The car swerved dangerously into the other lane before she got control again.

'Just shut up and drive, or I'll open you up. You hear me?'

It hurt to talk. Every time she opened her mouth, it pulled on the fresh wound and set a new rush of blood down her face. Her little brother was screaming. Katherine was screaming back, 'Shut up! Shut up!'

Maggie yelled over the chaos, 'All right! All right! I'll take you to Queensland, but we need to stop and get petrol, okay? We won't make it on an empty tank.'

Katherine growled and glowered, but she couldn't argue with the logic. They weren't going to get far without fuel.

On the edge of town, there was a petrol station, one of the last places that David had been sighted during his flight from Aberdeen. Maggie pulled into the station and silently fuelled up the car whilst Katherine sat immobile inside it. Her little brother was still in there. If she made any mistakes, if she gave any indication of what was going on, then Katherine could turn that butcher's knife on him. With the tank filled to the brim and as much of a delay as Maggie could muster to think, she headed inside to pay. The moment she was out of Katherine's sight, she ran for the till. 'Please, you've got to help me. Me and my brother. We've been kidnapped. It's Katherine Knight, she's got a knife. She wants me to drive her to Queensland. She did this to my face. Please. Call the police. Please.'

The police hadn't exactly been waiting for this call—they didn't even know that Katherine had been released from the hospital, or that it was possible for her to just sign herself out after she had been more or less incarcerated. Two officers rushed out to the petrol station, where things had already begun to deteriorate.

Maggie hadn't gone back to the car. She couldn't bring herself to get back in, even if it meant her little brother was in danger. Her cheek was throbbing with pain and her hands wouldn't stop shaking. Katherine's patience ran dry only a moment after Maggie went into the petrol station, but with no clear course of action to follow, she sat there growling and ranting to herself until the girl came back into sight.

The girl and the woman stared at each other for a long time, neither one of them willing to make the first move, but neither one of them willing to meet in the middle. That was when the boy in the back seat decided to take his chance. He unstrapped his belt and was halfway out the door before Katherine caught him by the back of his collar. When straining with all his strength proved insufficient to free him from her grasp, he wriggled out of his shirt and dropped to the tarmac with a yelp. Katherine was out of the car and on him before he could move more than a few feet towards his sister. The huge woman rode the boy down to the ground before placing the blade of the knife against his throat and dragging him to his feet by the hair. She nicked him once or twice in the scramble to their feet and little trails of red ran down his bare, dusty chest. Maggie covered her mouth to hold back a scream.

'Get over here and drive this car.'

Maggie shook her head. She didn't trust her own voice to work.

'You get over here or I'm going to gut him like a hog. You want to wear his guts? You want him dead? You're the one killing him, not me. Get over here, you little slut.'

This time, Maggie managed a little wail from between her fingers.

'You get in that car right this fucking minute or he's going to be squealing like a stuck pig, you hear me? I ain't going to kill him quick. It's going to hurt. You want to watch that? You want to hear that?'

She let out a little whimper, 'No.'

Maggie took a step forward, but the gruff old man from behind the counter had caught her by the arm. 'Don't do it.'

'I've got to,' she whimpered. 'You don't understand. He's my brother. I'm ... I'm meant to be taking care of him.'

He croaked back. 'If you give her what she wants, she doesn't need him anymore. She'll kill him. You stay away, or she'll kill him.'

The police car tore up the dirt road, throwing up a cloud of dust that blocked out the stars. Katherine spun on the spot, her sunken eyes tracking any movement, every bit the primeval predator that her doctors accused her of being. Her grip on the boy's hair never loosened, but the blade didn't bite any deeper, either. She was keeping her options open.

When the police came out of their car, it was with their hands held up. Both of them had been present for her arrest earlier in the week. They knew how dangerous this woman was and they didn't want to risk another innocent life being flung onto the train-tracks of her impending insanity. 'Let's just put that knife down now, eh? We're all friends here, aren't we Kath?'

She hissed, 'Fuck you and the mother you rode in on.'

'No need for that now, Kath.' They were more than used to the kind of venom that Katherine liked to spit. 'It's all over now, just you put that knife down and we can talk this through. No reason anyone needs to get in any trouble.'

'I'll slit his fucking throat. You take a step towards me and you're killing him.'

'Nobody is going nowhere, Kath. We're just standing here on a fine summer's evening, having ourselves a conversation.'

Katherine was not equipped to talk her way out of the situation and she couldn't fight with the boy in her arms. She made a snap decision, releasing him and kicking him towards the police in one fluid motion. 'Lucky little bitch.'

The situation shifted, one officer darting forward to drag the boy clear of Katherine, the other trying to circle around and place himself between her and the other civilians. Katherine went for him.

He got his arms up in time, and what could have been lethal or disfiguring blows just left nicks on his knuckles. The bellow that he let out was enough to startle her—similar enough to a bull being slaughtered— that for one moment she forgot where she was, the knife in her hand slipping into the next position of her deboning technique.

The policeman took his opportunity and tried to rush her, but she was too quick and too canny, even when her mind was completely elsewhere. She was the veteran of more bar-fights than could be counted, her body moved on its own, slamming a fist into his jaw and opening up his arm from elbow to wrist with the flashing tip of her knife. This time, the scream was definitely human. Katherine grinned.

With the boy safely stowed away in the car, the other Aberdeen policeman tried to creep up behind her, but he nearly caught her knife in the ribs for his trouble. They couldn't get close enough to subdue her, not when she had the knife. She spun from one of them to the other, her wild grin never faltering. Her eyes were dead, but she was laughing away the whole time that they were trying to arrest her. All of her life, she'd hidden this away inside of her. The vicious edge of Katherine that nobody ever wanted to see that only broke the surface when her mask of humanity was worn too thin.

The police were not equipped to deal with a problem like this. They were used to pulling apart the odd bar brawl—a maniac who'd spent her whole life training with a knife was a bit outside of their experience. Beyond that, their physical equipment wasn't up to the task, they had no reach on the huge woman, and that knife of hers could flick out and back so fast that they'd be more likely to lose a finger than make contact if they did try to hit her.

Once again, the petrol station attendant came to the rescue. He threw a pair of brooms that he'd been using to sweep up the forecourt to the police. Working together, they closed in on Katherine and managed to bat the knife out of her hands. Even with her disarmed, it still took both of them to wrestle her to the ground. She screamed, clawed and bit at them until she was handcuffed and even then she almost broke one officer's nose by flinging herself at him as they tried to wrestle her into the car.

This time, Katherine bypassed her old friends at St Elmo's and was sent directly to the high-security Morisset Psychiatric Hospital, where the correct paperwork was finally filed to restrain her movements until treatment could be proven to be effective. She remained in their care for almost a month.

Afterwards, she did not speak about her experience, but other residents of Morisset have shared plenty of horror stories about the quality of care that they received there. None of her usual manipulations were effective when she was taken outside the context of civilised society. The successes that she had achieved so far in her life were predicated almost entirely on everyone around her believing that she was normal, that her violent tendencies were just the run-of-the-mill outbursts of an ill-tempered woman. In Morisset, all of those deceptions fell away. When she was violent, they sedated her. When she was rude, they punished her. To begin with, she railed against it— spitting her medication in the faces of the staff, tearing her wafer-thin mattress to shreds and causing as much chaos as possible out of pure spite—but, before long, she fell back into the rhythm of institutionalisation, a pattern of behaviour that was all too familiar thanks to her upbringing under Ken's ironclad laws.

Her parents had no interest in fighting to see her freed. She had no friends. It would have been entirely possible for this to have been the final residence of Katherine Knight, if it hadn't been for the one man in all of the world who loved her.

Following her institutionalisation, it became clear to the staff of the hospital that David Kellet was in danger from Katherine. In her weekly therapy sessions, she had talked at great length about her desire for revenge against the man who had ruined her life, even detailing the fantasy that she had hoped to fulfil on the night when she had abducted and permanently scarred Maggie Macbeth.

She was going to drive to Queensland and torture David's mother until she gave Katherine his new address. Then, she was going to kill the old woman and hunt him down. She planned to kill him and the new girlfriend that she was certain he was with, along with any witnesses or bystanders who got in her way. Then, she was going to come back to Aberdeen and kill anyone who might have helped him in his escape, starting with the local mechanic who had recently fixed his car, allowing him to get away in the first place.

Patient and doctor confidentiality becomes moot when a patient is threatening to act on their violent impulses. The police were informed of her plans and took no time in tracking David down in Queensland and informing him of his still-wife's current mental state.

David was horrified by what he had done. He took all the blame for Katherine's actions on himself and drowned in self-loathing. Before the month was out, he had abandoned a second pregnant woman on the cusp of giving birth to one of his children. Along with his mother, another of Katherine's potential victims, David relocated back to Aberdeen, rejecting the new life that he had been building for himself in favour of returning to the waiting arms of a woman who desperately wanted him dead.

Once he had established himself back in Aberdeen and picked up his old job, he filed with the courts to have his wife released into his care, with both he and his mother offering to act as caretakers for the woman, ensuring that she would take her medication and do no harm to herself or others.

However dubious anyone who had followed the case of Katherine Knight up until this point may have been about the odds of their success, the decision was in the hands of the courts and the courts wanted as few able-bodied citizens of Australia confined in mental hospitals as possible.

On the 9th August 1976, Katherine was released into her husband's care, contingent on him ensuring that she continued to take the frankly ridiculous doses of antipsychotics and sedatives that had been prescribed to treat her condition. They drove straight from the hospital to Ken and Barbara's house to collect their daughter.

On arrival, David left Katherine and his mother in the car and went to get the baby himself. Katherine was still feeling fragile after everything that had happened to her in the last month and that was manifesting in a dark mood that filled both of her caretakers with fear. They quietly conferred before arriving at the elder Knight's farmhouse and decided that it would be for the best if Katherine didn't come face to face with the parents who had abandoned her in her hour of need. Katherine did not handle abandonment well, and they wanted to keep her as calm as possible. Any violent outbursts could have led to a more permanent return to Morisset, and all three of them knew it.

When David knocked on the door, it wasn't Ken who answered. He'd been afraid it would be Ken, afraid that this would turn into a physical altercation that he was certain he wouldn't win, but instead, he was confronted with silly, old Barbara. She lunged at him and caught him by the hair. 'What did you do to my daughter you cheating piece of sheep shit?'

David was so surprised that she barrelled him right off his feet. He tumbled backwards, with her fingernails scraping over his scalp as she tried to keep her grip. 'You destroyed my Katy. You drove her crazy. You just couldn't keep your dick in your trousers, could you? You had to ruin everything!'

She started stamping on him as he lay there on the gravel path and, whilst she lacked her daughter's size, she had the same tenacity and cruel aim when it came to kicking a man when he was down.

Katherine came storming up the path so fast that David's mother didn't even have a chance to shout out a warning, let alone try to stop her. Her fist caught Barbara under the chin, sending the old woman flying back to her own doorstep. 'Don't you ever lay a hand on David again! He saved me. You left me to rot and he came back for me.' A predatory growl crept into her voice. 'He's mine! Mine! You never even look at him again!'

Katherine stepped right over her bleeding mother and strolled into the house. She moved from room to room like she was in a dream, picking up everything that belonged to the baby as she went until finally, she found Melissa, fast asleep in her father's arms. He handed the baby over without a word of admonishment, without even a hint that he was surprised to see her, either.

Then, as fast as they'd descended on the house, they were gone. Zooming off down the dirt roads back to the little flat David had been renting by the meat-works. A home that would only last them a few days more, before change swept through their lives again.

Katherine could not stand the stares of the people around town and whatever benefits to her mental stability the familiarity of Aberdeen might have brought, were grossly outweighed by the terrible memories that she had of the town. David had no attachment to the place. His mother had only lived there a couple of weeks and already loathed it. All of the spite that Katherine used to fling at David seemed to have been burned away by the fires of the tribulations that she had been through in the last month. Either that or harshly curbed by the medication which had her moving through a hazy world devoid of sharp edges. She was every bit the loving, pliant wife that David had always hoped she would be, so when she begged him in tears to take her away from this horrible place, where their worst moments had been, he didn't have to be asked twice.

The couple relocated to Woodridge, a quiet suburb of Brisbane, where neither one of them had any family ties, nor where there was any way that whispers could follow them. His mother continued to live with them and, with that addition to the household, Katherine realised that her presence within the house was almost entirely unnecessary. All of the cooking and cleaning naturally passed along to the older woman and, after the first few months, even the care of Melissa became just another of her mother-in-law's chores.

With all the hours of the day to fill, Katherine started a job hunt and it wasn't long before she picked up a new job on the line at the Dinmore meat-works in nearby Ipswich. She took to the work like a fish to water and, before long, she had fallen back into her old rhythm, surprising her new employers and co-workers with her skill with the custom knives that she had brought along from her old job. Knives that she would spend a solid ten minutes sharpening before every shift.

She remained on her medication, which slowed her down a little, but that also meant that the number of 'incidents' in the workplace remained relatively low. She would still inflict complicated schemes of revenge upon anyone who crossed her, but they were more often practical jokes rather than violent outbursts. In her home life, all of the pressure to be perfect around the home had been removed thanks to the assistance of her mother-in-law, and the extra money she was bringing in gave them a more comfortable buffer between their regular life and bankruptcy. She was living the kind of life that she had always dreamed of living, with a loyal husband, a happy baby and all of the support she could ever have wanted. She was miserable.

The only moments in her life when she was happy were when she was cutting into the meat of some slaughtered animal or when she was on the long, silent drive back to Woodridge after a day at work. Even that was only a treat because sometimes an animal would stray onto the road and she could swerve to hit it. She had gone from being the little girl who saved injured animals and nursed them back to health to being the killer of animals of all shapes and sizes. Every time she heard bones splintering against the grill of her car, that old, wicked smile crept back over her face. The old Katherine was still there, just under the surface, lost but not forgotten.

The Dark Knight Returns

Katherine sank into the dull monotony of her new life, doing her best to forget everything that had happened to her and that she had done. To her neighbours in suburbia, she barely even drew attention. In Aberdeen, she had been a legend, the subject of fear and ridicule but known to everyone. Out here, she felt like she was invisible, like she was fading away. For years she went through the same repetitive motions, rising with the dawn, driving to work, slicing her way through another day before turning back and mechanically delivering all of the things that David Kellet needed to convince himself that his wife actually loved him. One of those mechanical deliveries of affection came to fruition on the 6th March 1980, in the form of Natasha Maree Kellet, the second of Katherine's children.

David stayed by Katherine's side throughout the whole of her labour, driving her to the hospital and holding her hand through every grunt and strain. Neither one of them spoke about the birth of their last daughter or the darkness that had followed. Neither one of them was so foolish as to dig up the past when it already haunted their every waking moment.

Katherine took time off work to be with her baby and soon found that her mother-in-law was an intrusion rather than a help. This time, she felt that she had the opportunity to get things right. This time, she could bond with her baby, have the kind of relationship that she had always wanted to have with her own mother, but Old Mrs Kellet always seemed to be in her way. Eventually, given the options of a violent outburst or going back to work, Katherine elected to go back to doing the one thing she had ever been praised for. She sank back into that routine like she hoped it would drown her, but the distractions of work, roadkill and family life were never enough.

She was constantly bored out of her mind. All of the things that used to bring her joy had become numbed and even the satisfaction of her work never seemed to reach her. The treacherous voice that exists inside of all of us, demanding that we destroy our lives and go back to the freedom we knew before, wasn't a whisper in Katherine's mind, it was a primal scream. Her thoughts were dominated by fantasies of escape from this mediocre life and, before long, that resentment began to turn outwards. She grew colder and colder towards David, completely ignored his mother—who still lived in the house with them—and even her precious children began to receive the same treatment.

On Natasha Maree's fourth birthday, Katherine's misery came to a head. Four years after the birth of her first daughter, she'd had Natasha to look forward to, but now there was nothing. She packed up her things the next day, collected the children and drove back to Aberdeen.

David's abandonment of her had been one of the most catastrophic and defining events in her entire life. An event that loomed so large in her mental landscape that it had threatened to kill her and a half-dozen others. Yet, her abandonment of David was almost casual, like she was discarding some tawdry thing that she just didn't need anymore. David was upset, of course, but at the same time, he was relieved. He could see the clues that the old Katherine was clawing her way back to the surface and, as much as he may have loved his idea of Katherine

Knight, the reality that had seared a line into his face and smashed his skull was too frightening to forget.

For the first month back home in Aberdeen, Katherine and the children stayed with her parents, out of sight of the town gossips in the countryside. She filed for a divorce, which David didn't even try to contest in a startling display of self-preservation that seemed entirely out of character.

Shortly after the divorce was granted, Katherine rented a small house in nearby Muswellbrook and picked up her old job in the Aberdeen meat-works again, as if she had never left. Eight years had passed since she laid down her knives and spiralled into madness, but for her, it was like yesterday.

Tragedy struck only two years after her return to work in Aberdeen. Whilst she was hefting the carcass of a particularly heavy hog, Katherine injured her back. She was rushed to the hospital by her supervisor, but the damage was already done. The wear and tear of her job and the rough life she had lived had put an end to her career working in the abattoir. The heavy lifting that the job required might have been possible for her once or twice a day, despite her injury, but each repetition would have just made her condition worsen. The job that had been the only constant in her life, the only truly good thing, was over.

She was put on to a disability pension and filed for workplace compensation through her union representative, and the government provided her with a Housing Commission apartment on the outskirts of Aberdeen, as she no longer needed to be in close proximity to the abattoir.

In 1986, Katherine turned 31 and realised that she still had another thirty years or more stretched out ahead of her. Her kids were pretty poor company, although she had done her best to patch up the relationships that she had left to rot for so long when they lived with their father. Melissa was old enough to truly understand her mother by this point and became the friend and confidant that her mother had always hoped for. Katherine shared all of the gruesome details of her life with her daughter but made sure not to repeat her own mother's mistake of reinforcing them as the natural order of things. She warned Melissa about men in no uncertain terms, but she also acknowledged her own loneliness, even if she didn't quite have the vocabulary to really explain it to her daughter.

In the evenings, Katherine began leaving Melissa in charge of her little sister and going out to bars again. She didn't return to the height of her youthful exploits, spending as much time just listening to the bustle around her as wading into every argument, but that was likely because she no longer felt like she had a group to belong to. The abattoir had always had a high rate of employee attrition and the men who came drinking from there each night were almost all strangers to Katherine.

But then again, strangers were really what she needed— people who had never heard the stories about her. All the older folk of Aberdeen had kept her reputation alive in her absence and whatever notions of dating she might have been entertaining soon vanished in the face of the town's long memory. Anyone who knew who she was by reputation alone fled from her, leaving only the company of a few outcasts and stragglers who remembered her from before Melissa was born, a decade before.

Luckily for Katherine, not everyone who drank in Aberdeen was from Aberdeen. Thirty-eight-year-old David Saunders worked in the nearby mines and liked to come into town for a drink after a long shift down in the darkness. He mostly kept to himself—he was more than a little socially awkward after a lifetime of isolation and back-breaking labour—so he wasn't privy to all of the stories about Katherine. When she approached him in the bar one night, it was like a dream come true for him. She had started wearing thick glasses and, over the years, the sun had done its wearing work on the skin of her face, but her red hair made every freckle seem like an addition rather than an imperfection. More pressingly for a man like David, she had lost her waifish figure after years of work and replaced it with a toned body that she wasn't shy about showing off. Combined with the way that she was predatorily sexual, he thought that he had hit the jackpot.

She took him home with her that first night and, within a month, he had more or less abandoned his own apartment in nearby Scone in favour of living with her full-time. Home-cooked meals and a family that he could slot into like a missing puzzle piece—David had never been happier in all his life. When the other men in the mine realised who he was dating and started trying to warn him off, he didn't believe a word of it. He convinced himself that they were speaking out of jealousy or spite. Even when they recounted the whole story of her abduction of the Macbeth children, he claimed it was just a misunderstanding. He hadn't seen any sign that Katherine, his beloved Katherine, could have done anything like the horrible things that they were describing. At least, not at first.

They would fight relatively frequently. Katherine was suspicious of his movements when he wasn't with her. After work, he still went for the odd drink and sometimes the shifts in the mine were irregular, depending on how rich the veins they uncovered happened to be. She would accuse him of philandering at the slightest provocation, but he took it all in good humour. He could tell that Katherine had a fiery temper, but even when the screaming was at a fever pitch, he never really felt any danger; after all, she was just a woman.

Sometimes she would throw him out and he'd go sleep in his flat in Scone for a night or two before she showed up, begging his forgiveness and lavishing him with so much affection he barely knew how to respond. He kept a few bare essentials in his old apartment, but the majority of his clothes and belongings came with him to Katherine's government-supplied house.

On the anniversary of their first meeting, he returned home from work with a little bunch of flowers purchased in town, expecting a feast laid out and a night of exertions on par with every other. Instead, he found Katherine in a dark mood. She tossed the flowers aside without even looking at them and continued her pacing around the tiny kitchen.

A few weeks before, David had bought a dog for his new family. The girls had been delighted, with Natasha, in particular, being completely smitten with what she called 'the dingo pup.' Katherine didn't seem to care too much for the animal one way or the other, but she tolerated its presence in her back garden as a small price to pay for Natasha's delight. Still, she always made sure to call it 'David's dog' rather than accepting it as a part of the family.

He tried talking to her, tried to tease the reason for her foul mood out, but she just kept pacing around the kitchen, slamming cupboards and chopping vegetables in sporadic bursts of fury. He had almost given up when she suddenly darted out of the back door. David followed after her, profoundly confused about what was going on until he heard the pitiful squealing outside. Katherine had the puppy by the scruff of its neck, dangling it by a fistful of fur and skin, level to her eyes. It was letting out a piteous wail that kept distracting David, but she did nothing else until he looked at her. Then, the chopping knife in her hand flashed out and the bleeding started. She slit the dog's throat, so deeply that he could see its spine glinting white in the mess of gore. Its wails turned to gurgles, then to dreadful silence as she dropped it to the ground.

'If I ever catch you running around on me, that is what I'll do to you.'

David backed away from her, horrified. She dropped the knife into the dog's corpse to stand on end, then stalked after him. He backed into the kitchen, babbling, 'I'd never be unfaithful to you, Kath! You have to believe me. I've never even looked at another woman since you came along. Never.'

Her eyes narrowed, but she couldn't really see him, not now that the red rage had descended over her vision. He was just a shape now, a looming shadow that she poured all of her rage into. She snatched up a frying pan and swung for him. He managed to get an arm up in time, but the heavy iron hit even that with so much force that his bones cracked. She brought it down on him again and again as he curled up in a ball, his piteous screams not much different from the sounds his dog had made. Eventually, she tired, dropped the pan and dropped to her knees beside him. 'Why did you do it, David? Why would you do that to me and our family? Why?'

He could not answer, he had been knocked unconscious.

Once he had regained consciousness, he spent a week in his own apartment in Scone, ignoring the phone, refusing to answer the door and only scurrying outside for long enough to resupply with medicinal whiskey for the pain, or to work a short shift down in the mines once the worst of the bruising had subsided. He had never been a fearful man before, willing to wade into dangerous stretches of tunnel where other miners feared to tread, but now he flinched at every bump and bang of equipment. The other men began to make a joke of his twitchiness, but some of the older natives of Aberdeen did their best to curb that mockery. They knew what Katherine was capable of doing to a man—many of their number had been on the receiving end of her fists through the years.

She ambushed him on his way home from work one night, camped out in front of his apartment door. He was paralysed with fear the moment that she came into sight. She wept. She sobbed. She threw herself on the ground at his feet, begging him to forgive her and, fool that he was, he did. Everyone deserved a second chance in David Saunders' mind and, as far as he could see, from the broken woman in front of him, Katherine had a moment of madness that she didn't deserve to lose the love of her life over.

He'd made a few mistakes in his life and been grateful for the forgiveness and as she dragged him into his flat and stripped off their clothes, he realised just how grateful Katherine was going to be.

The honeymoon period lasted for a couple of months before Katherine started to draw back from David all over again, vanishing back into her own mind and slipping into the self-destructive patterns that were ingrained there. It would have been just a matter of time before her internal turmoil exploded outwards in the form of violence again, if it hadn't been for a lucky coincidence.

Katherine was pregnant again and, for David, that changed everything. He got rid of his flat in Scone and put down the deposit on a house. It was a tiny two-bedroom weatherboard house on MacQueen Street in Aberdeen, not much to look at from the outside and dark and dismal on the inside. Its flaws aside, it was the first home that Katherine had ever truly owned any part of and she adored it. She had spent her entire life in other people's houses, in rented apartments and homes that belonged to authority figures. For the first, time she felt like she was free to make someplace her own, like she wasn't just passing through. She set to work immediately, decorating every surface of the walls and even the ceilings with her own special brand of interior design. Animal pelts, taxidermy, skulls, rusty animal traps, leather jackets, machetes, rakes, boots, pitchforks and, of course, her beloved knives, covered every inch of the tiny house. Just brushing against a wall was liable to give you tetanus.

Sarah was born in June of 1988 and David had absolutely no warning of how the arrival of the baby was going to affect Katherine. She fell almost immediately into another downward spiral of depression, trapped in her memories surrounding the birth of Melissa and the chaos that had followed. He went on with his life, oblivious to the doom that was swiftly approaching, unaware of how little it would take to push Katherine over the edge into violence once more.

In early 1989, when their relationship had deteriorated, to the point that Katherine was barely even speaking to him, her worker's compensation finally came through in a lump sum. It was more money than she had ever seen in her life and she knew exactly what she wanted to do with it. She paid off the house on MacQueen Street, essentially buying the house out from under David. The house had been the only thing that Katherine stood to lose if she lashed out at him, and now, with that last tenuous restraint severed, his time was up.

As Katherine had grown colder, David's temper had begun to flare up. Where before he would have accepted any treatment from a woman, his brief taste of domestic bliss at the beginning of their relationship had now spoiled him. When housework was left untouched, he shouted at her. When the baby was left filthy and untended, he shouted at her. One day, in 1989, he returned home to find that all of his clothes were dirty. Katherine hadn't bothered to do the washing all week. It was the proverbial straw that broke the camel's back. He bellowed for Katherine and when she finally sulked into the room, he pointed at the heap of dirty clothes. 'Will you do something about this? It's been sitting there all week whilst you've done nothing.'

She turned on her heel and stalked out of the room, returning just a moment later with scissors in her hand. She held up one of his shirts and started cutting. Through the first shirt, he just stood there in shock. Through the second, he flushed with rage and, when she hefted the only pair of trousers he had without holes in the knees, he darted forward to snatch them.

He stopped abruptly with his hands still reaching out for the denim. At first, he couldn't understand what had happened. He couldn't understand where the pain was coming from. Then, he looked down and saw the scissors jammed into his stomach. The blood spreading out in a perfect circle across his gut. He looked up into Katherine's eyes, expecting to see surprise or horror at the accident that had just happened, but her eyes were merciless and dark, like she was staring right through him to a future that he didn't feature in.

She twisted the scissors as she yanked them out, and it set David howling. Shock kicked in, numbing the pain and giving him the precious moments that he needed to ensure his survival.

Katherine had dropped the bloody scissors and was fumbling for her trusty iron to finish the job. David didn't hang around long enough to give her the chance. He ran for his life, leaping into his car and tearing right out of Aberdeen without pause.

The stab wound in his gut proved to be superficial, missing any vital organs by sheer luck, but David knew that he wouldn't be so lucky a third time. He rented a room in Scone for a few nights, returning to Aberdeen for only as long as it took to file for a leave of absence from his job in the mine. His foreman had been brought up on tales of Katherine Knight. He didn't have to be asked twice before he gave David the leave he needed to escape her.

It was almost three months later when he returned to Aberdeen to try and rescue his daughter from Katherine's clutches. He even entertained the idea of trying to rescue her other daughters, too. Surely they had spent enough time with their mother that they recognised the danger they were in? He never even made it into town before the police pulled him over. There was an outstanding Apprehended Violence Order against him, something like a restraining order with more immediate legal consequences, filed by Katherine on the day that he left and outlining a long history of domestic abuse on his part. David was given two options, leave town immediately or go to jail. He chose to leave and, thanks to the AVO outstanding against him, he didn't have a hope of securing custody of Sarah or access to the house that he had paid the deposit for. Katherine had won again.

The Last Survivor

John Chillingworth came back into Katherine's life towards the end of 1989. He had lived an entire life in the time since he had last seen her working the line in the Aberdeen meat-works. Shortly after rejecting the teenaged Knight, he'd met a more stable, if less exciting, woman and married her in short order, moving away to the city for almost a decade before his ever-worsening drinking problem led him to make one stupid decision too many. He arrived back in Aberdeen freshly divorced and more than halfway to being pickled in alcohol. A bit of luck at the abattoir meant that the new supervisor had once been his co-worker and, instead of the miserable remnants of a man slumped in the chair in front of the interviewer, his younger self was recalled—The John Chillingworth who would always pick up an extra shift and help his co-workers with the tricky jobs. His next stop after securing the job was to pop into the housing office, where he was offered an apartment in spitting distance of the slaughterhouse. His third and final stop was the bar in town, where he fully intended to drain the last dregs of his savings before he had to report for work on Monday.

Katherine was there. Waiting for him like a memory brought to life. He was still ten years her senior, but now that she was no longer a teenager, it seemed to be less of an impediment than it once had. John was appallingly bad at taking care of himself, having leaned heavily on his wife to handle even the most basic functions of his life so that he could focus on the two pillars that he hung his personality on: working and drinking.

As a teenager, Katherine's raunchy flirting had been uncomfortable, almost comical, but as a full-grown woman, it had become intensely appealing to John Chillingworth. The two of them remembered each other well and, over a night of heavy drinking, he eventually confided in her just how tempted he had been by her offers all those years ago. Offers that she was more than happy to present to him again in short order.

He didn't even sleep for one night in the barracks housing that had been provided to him. Katherine took him home with her to MacQueen Street and whatever horror he might have felt when he looked at the horrific decorations that coated the inside of that dwelling were soon forgotten at the first glimpse of her naked flesh. In a strange way, he was the perfect fit for Katherine Knight. His drinking brought all of his animal instincts to the fore and stripped away any need for the kind of complex conversation that she was so uncomfortable with. They fucked, he went to work, he drank, and they fucked again. Sometimes she'd provide him with a meal in between and sometimes he'd hand over whatever change was left from his paycheque after he'd settled his bar tab. It wasn't the formal arrangements that Katherine had become accustomed to, but it suited her well, appealing to that savage part of her psyche that just wanted with immediacy.

None of the men that Katherine had pursued through the years could have been called soft—her tastes had been shaped to the mould of tough guys like her father—and, whilst she liked to physically dominate her lovers, that didn't mean that she could abide any sign of weakness in them. Despite all of that, the men she had dated all seemed to be relatively soft in the grand scale of things. They had lived as sheltered a life as the time and place of their births would have allowed and their instincts were those of civilised men. Chillingworth was different. The exact details of the traumas that had driven him to drink have been lost to history, but they had left him with a very different set of responses when confronted with conflict to the startled 'deer in headlights' approach of the Davids that Katherine had been dating before. He had a survivor's instincts. When he was pushed, he would push back. He had experienced enough pain in his life to know that it doesn't end without somebody ending it.

When Katherine first threw a tantrum at him for an imagined affair with another woman, he had sat through the foul language and flying spittle without flinching, a bemused expression on his face that just enraged her even more.

When Katherine took a swing at his face, he ducked under it and countered it with a quick slap that left her ears ringing. She had thrown him out of the house for that, startled and unsure what to do when confronted with a victim who wouldn't just sit there and take the abuse that she felt compelled to dole out.

John spent his first night in his assigned barracks apartment after that argument, but by morning, Katherine was there begging him to return to their cosy little arrangement and lavishing him with the sort of attention that he had spent his whole life starved of.

The house on MacQueen Street was always loud, always busy. Katherine didn't much care that her children heard her screaming arguments, or her equally deafening lovemaking, and it didn't take long for John to adapt to the racket. He spent all day surrounded by the squealing of animals being slaughtered; a houseful of kids crammed into a spare room was hardly worse than that, even if they were a little more persistent.

By this point, Melissa was fifteen years old and had already left school to begin dating men up to five years her senior, much to Katherine's delight. She spent only a small fraction of her nights sleeping in the house and when she did, she was forced to share a bed with her younger sisters. Circumstances had forced her to mature much faster than her peers and, by 1990, she was treated as more or less an equal by her mother. A friend. Which was why, when she heard about his one tiny act of violence against her mother, she was enraged. She confronted John, screaming in his face, her own countenance turning the same bright red that characterised her mother's rages. John was halfway past drunk and having none of it. He slapped Melissa just as he had done her mother.

It was Melissa's first brush with first-hand violence, beyond her mother's attempts on her life, which she was too young to remember. It shut her up promptly and ended the argument permanently.

Katherine fell pregnant again, at about the same time that all of this was coming to a head. John made some noises about making their arrangement a little more official at the time, but when he realised that Katherine wasn't going to push him for a marriage proposal, he didn't press further. He was already living with her and doing as much as he would have done for her as a husband—he didn't see the point of doing any more.

He was not prepared for the emotional tempest that surrounded pregnancy in the mind of Katherine Knight. Her occasional accusations of infidelity went from a monthly occurrence to an hourly one. After her screaming rages, he would often just leave the house rather than have to deal with a pregnant woman getting physical with him, spending his evenings drinking and then sleeping it off in his apartment.

It wasn't long before this pattern became apparent to the women of Aberdeen. Despite his age and his drinking, John was still considered to be an attractive man. He had become accustomed to having certain needs fulfilled by Katherine that she was no longer in any sort of mood to entertain, so before long he began to do the thing that she accused him of. He didn't go on a campaign of conquests or anything so vulgar, but once his judgement was sufficiently impaired by alcohol and attractive women started falling all over him, a certain inevitability set in.

Towards the end of 1990, Katherine gave birth to her first and only son, Eric. His father was present at the birth and offered all of the support that he could muster. Almost instantly, all of the imagined sins that Katherine had heaped at his door were forgiven and he was welcomed back into the family home with open arms. This new, maternal Katherine was one that John had never seen before, but he liked it. She was the domestic goddess that had lured in her previous partners and the gentle, loving wife that had kept them ensnared even when her violent tendencies began to show. John was completely taken in.

He was so taken in by the illusion of softness and kindness that his conscience began to nip at him. He had been unfaithful to Katherine at a time when she was feeling her most vulnerable and if he didn't make it right then he knew that guilt was going to drive him right back down to the bottom of a bottle and make his whole life fall apart. So, he confessed.

Katherine's rages had always been incandescent, but this one burned with a cold fire that should have served as a warning in itself. She walked calmly through to the bathroom and punched the glass containing John's false teeth into fragments, with the enamel teeth scattering over the yellowed tile in a chatter.

Even then, John didn't grasp the depth of the trouble that he was in. 'Oh look what you've done, now. I've only got the one pair I'm wearing to last me 'til I get those fixed.'

Katherine eyed him up, then swung her fist again. Breaking the set of false teeth in the jar had been an inconvenience to him. Breaking the set that was still in his mouth was a lesson. He spat out the fragments along with a mouthful of blood. There was no fear on his face. If that was what she'd been hoping for, she had grossly misjudged the man. Instead, there was a careful, assessing expression. He was a survivor, and he was calculating his odds.

That night, he slept in his own apartment, but the next day, he came back to the house to collect his things. That was when he found her lying nearly-dead from an overdose of sleeping pills on the bed. Just like that, he was ensnared again. He panicked, snatched her up and drove her to the hospital. Her stomach was pumped and she was saved, but she ended up back in a mental institution for observation for a week, to ensure that the threat of suicide had passed. During that time, Chillingworth watched her children and drove out to see her through every visiting hour. He was horrified by what he had driven her to and all of his safety concerns faded away in the face of the reality of losing her over his own foolish choices. When she was released, his apology was accepted and life returned to the same strange equilibrium it had before. John thought that life was getting back to normal, but he did not realise that the proverbial Sword of Damocles was hanging over his head.

The broad strokes of the legend of Katherine Knight had been preserved in Chillingworth's absence, easy enough for him to pick up from anyone he wanted to talk to in town. The specific details of the horrors that she had wrought on Aberdeen were less readily available. Everyone thought to warn John about the murder attempts on her previous partners, the near-death of her baby and her commitment to a mental hospital, but nobody thought to warn him about her long memory, or the months or years she would wait to spring an ice-cold revenge on those who'd wronged her.

She memorised his schedule every single day. She knew exactly where he was going to be at any given time and, on those nights when he went to the bar, which was most of them, she knew exactly when her old friend the bartender would gently nudge the man towards the door. When he came home from the bar after a long night at work and found her spread-eagled on the bed with another man thrusting away between her legs, he knew that it was deliberate. She had chosen to make him see that, to see her affair right in front of his eyes. To know that it could have been going on for months or years without him ever knowing until this moment when she wanted him to know. He was done.

He left the house and never came back. It took him less than a week to put his affairs in order, during which time he was lucky enough to avoid Katherine, who considered him to be sulking and nothing more.

After his brush with Katherine Knight, John Chillingworth got his life back in order. He moved to the big city, joined a program, quit drinking and eventually got a full-time job as a counsellor, helping addicts who were trying to break free from the cycle of brutality and addiction. Out of all the partners that Katherine Knight chose for herself, he was the only one to escape without permanent injury and it seems that he wanted to pay that good karma forwards to the other men in the world who might have been in similarly dire straits.

Unfortunately, there was nothing that he could do to help a man who was already in the clutches of a dangerous and self-destructive addiction but completely unwilling to try to get out on his own. There was no saving a man like John Price.

The High Price of Living

John Price, known as 'Pricey' to his friends, was the man that John Chillingworth had caught Katherine in bed with. Their affair had been going on for almost a year before Katherine decided to use him as a blunt instrument of vengeance against her partner, but as uncomfortable as he was with the whole situation, it wasn't enough to keep him away from Katherine. He was a grown man with a less than amicable divorce in his past. In 1988, he had split from his wife, leaving her to raise their two-year-old daughter but taking his two older children with him to Aberdeen.

He was well-respected in the community of Aberdeen and well-liked by everyone that he met—a real rarity in such a small town. Pricey even had a good reputation in the mine, where he was known for his skill as a first-aider, one of the first responders whenever there was an accident down in the dark beneath the hills. There was something in Pricey that brought out the best in Katherine. Even when it seemed that their sexually-charged affair was transforming into something more stable, he was able to guide her gently into that next phase without any outbursts. She met with his two children, Becky and Little John, and was surprised to find that they liked her. Her own children were very taken with the new, gentler man that their mother had taken up with. In normal circumstances, it would have been an ideal situation, but there was nothing normal about Katherine and John's relationship.

Just as she always had in the past, she soon began accusing John of infidelity. Just as she always had in the past, her screaming and cursing turned to violence—although it was more restrained now than it had been with the men in her past. She did not jump straight to acts of outright brutality for fear of losing Price, just as she had Chillingworth. It is possible that she was not restraining herself but that she was merely mellowing as middle age swept in; just one look at her proved that this was not the case, though. The red flush that had once marked her berserk tantrums had now permanently discoloured her face, like she was trapped in that state permanently. A visible warning to anyone who met her of the personality hidden behind those bottle-thick glasses.

John took all of her aggression in his stride, for the most part. He'd already been through a cold and loveless marriage and he generally interpreted her assaults as signs that she was passionate about him. It was also difficult for him to take her concerns about infidelity as anything more than slightly flattering jealousy, since it was clear to everyone that he was completely devoted to her and smitten, to boot.

Warnings about Katherine Knight had not fallen on deaf ears when it came to John, but with rose-tinted glasses on, he tended to interpret events differently from those who'd lived through them. He adopted Katherine's version of events wherein she was a victim, struggling back against an unfair and oppressive system and any parts of her story that weren't protected under that dubious interpretation he fed into his own delusions of machismo. The men who had come before him were weak and that was why they considered Katherine's passions to be something worthy of fear. He was strong, so he could weather the storm and receive his just rewards on the other side of each frenzy.

By 1993, even her ranting and raging on that subject of infidelity had begun to fade in favour of a new argument. She wanted to know, if he was so devoted to her, why he wouldn't propose marriage.

In John's mind, marriage was the end of happiness. He'd had a healthy and happy relationship with his first wife before they got married and from what he could gather about Katherine's first husband, he got the very same impression about their relationship. If they could live a happy life together, then why did they need to go and put the stamp of doom on their relationship by announcing it as formal in front of friends, family and the government?

After two years of the same question, answered a dozen times with varying degrees of bellowing, John decided to take their relationship to the next level and get her off his back. In 1995, he invited Katherine and her children to come and live with him and his. He was a supervisor up at the mine, running shifts on his own most of the time and, as a result, he was making good money doing a job that he genuinely enjoyed. That, in turn, had led to a good house, one with enough rooms that all of Katherine's kids wouldn't have to be piled up in a single bed at night. With his three-bedroom bungalow on St Andrews Street, it would have been madness for her to refuse the offer of such a comfortable life, but she still wasn't willing to give up her own little nightmare home on MacQueen Street. In the end, John didn't force the issue. His prosperity was so assured that he didn't need Katherine to sell her house to make sharing his home economically viable. The strange collection of skins and bones were left hanging in her empty house, whilst everything that lived came to stay with John in his.

For almost a year, they were in a honeymoon period. Her pointless, petty arguments all seemed to have been crushed by his invitation to live with him. They lived as if they were married and, indeed, under common-law, they were considered to be a married couple. The children all got on well with each other and Katherine became increasingly maternal towards John's kids, too. It seemed like a fairy-tale relationship where nothing could go wrong. Then, she started asking him to marry her again.

The arguments went on and on without a moment's respite for either one of them, but whilst they exhausted John, fighting just seemed to give Katherine more energy. It was like she took some twisted delight in badgering and harassing him, day in and day out. It went on and on for a year, ever-worsening until eventually, in 1998, she went too far.

The mine had recently replaced all of their first aid kits, tossing the rest into a dumpster to be destroyed, but the thrifty John Price had lifted them out of the trash and brought them home. Their contents may have been past their 'best by' date, but the majority of them were still perfectly functional and he wasn't in the habit of getting rid of something that could still save a life.

One day, whilst he was at work, Katherine took the video camera that he'd bought her for Christmas and filmed all of the kits, providing a running commentary about all of the things that John stole from his workplace. With the same deranged grin on her red face that she always displayed during her most self-destructive acts of cruelty, she mailed the tape to his bosses at the mine.

By the end of the week, John's entire life had fallen apart. The job that he had spent his whole adult life working had fired him for stealing company property. Even after the situation was fully explained, they didn't care. It seemed to be a punishment for associating with characters like Katherine Knight as much as it was retribution for any theft.

He drove home from the mine, gathered up all of Katherine's things and threw them out into the street. When she arrived home, she found that the locks were changed. They stood on the doorstep and had a screaming argument for upwards of two hours before, finally, on threat of police involvement, she snatched up her belongings and stormed off back to her little house on MacQueen Street.

It was like a weight was lifted from John. No longer would he have to endure the insane demands and ramblings of that woman. Even if it had taken the loss of everything else in his life, at least now he was free of her.

Work was never easy to come by in Aberdeen and men found that, unless one mining company hired you out from under the nose of another, there was little chance of employment underground. There was no official blacklist, but people talked and none of them wanted a thing to do with Katherine Knight or any of her men. Nobody wanted to invite that chaos into their lives or their businesses. The whole town knew what Katherine had done to him and, whilst there was some sympathy and pity, there was just as much contempt. They'd warned him about Katherine Knight and he'd still gone along with her like a fool.

He didn't even care that they looked down on him; he was just glad to be free of her. The pay was terrible but he found work at the abattoir before the month was out. His savings were depleted and the big house was now a massive strain on his finances, but even if he had to tighten his belt, he was going to survive.

Of course, it wasn't long before Katherine crossed his path again. She still lingered on the periphery of the meat-works crowd more often than not and whilst, she'd avoided the alcoholism that plagued Aberdeen up until this point, she had now turned to the bottle, just as her father had before her.

Every night she was in the bar, just out of sight, like a memory lingering on the edges of John's life. Every time that he saw her, he remembered the good times that they'd shared. He remembered the kindness and the love. After a few weeks without attention from another woman, he started to recall the carnal aspects of their relationship with some affection, too. With the kind of animal cunning normally only reserved for ambush predators, Katherine waited until he approached her before she sprung her trap.

By the time the clock struck midnight, she was back in his bed and their relationship had resumed the intensity that had tricked him into forgetting all of the stories about her the first time around. But, even that proved insufficient when the cold light of dawn shone over them.

Katherine had expected to move back into the house immediately, to pick up right where she had left off. John wasn't as foolish as that. He might have let her back into his life and into his bed, but he wasn't inviting her to live with him any time soon.

Despite that little bit of distance, the story of their reconciliation swept through Aberdeen before midday and it wasn't even the end of his working day before John was confronted by a group of his friends with an ultimatum. They had no intention of watching him destroy himself. They refused to just stand by and watch as he ruined the life he had struggled so hard to put back on track once he had rid himself of that 'devil woman.' For as long as he took up with Katherine Knight, they were going to have nothing to do with him. His calls would go unanswered and his friendships would go untended until they went their separate ways.

Even with that ultimatum delivered, his friends still didn't truly abandon him. It pained them to see him putting himself through the same torments over and over, so they reached out to the only person that they thought he might listen to. David Kellet.

Katherine's first husband had been in hiding ever since the relationship broke down and age was starting to wear heavily on him after the hard life he'd led. The scar on his face was still angry and red, hot to the touch. He approached John in the bar one night when he was sat alone drinking. He'd been called back into town by his old friends to add his experience to their warnings.

He told John every single story that he could remember, illustrating each one with a new scar. He warned the man that Katherine Knight was not to be trifled with, sharing the warning that he'd received on his own wedding day. 'If you cross her, she'll kill you. Do you understand? This isn't a joke. She will kill you.'

It was obvious from the bemused smile on John's face that he wasn't getting through to him, so David bade his sad farewells to his old friends and took to the road before Katherine had a chance to hear that he was in town. He still lived in fear of her, even decades after their relationship had ended. He still woke up gasping for air and scrabbling at his throat. She haunted his nightmares.

Life fell into a new routine, with Katherine in a state of limbo, allowed to come into John's house to cook for him, or for what they termed 'date nights,' but never allowed to overstay her welcome or feel settled. Her old arguments about marriage fell by the wayside as she demanded more and more frequently that he let her and her children move back in. The kids had been welcomed back into John's home with open arms—he had never held them responsible for their mother's actions, even when she tried to use them as the justification for them. Even spending every other night in his bed, Katherine was still uncertain of her place. She wanted his house to be hers again. It isn't clear whether she entertained ideas of taking it from him when their relationship finally degenerated or if she was not thinking that far ahead. Once again, that animal desire for comfort was winning out over whatever more complex motives she might have possessed. And that desire was being thwarted at every turn.

This went on and on, escalating from harassing questions to screaming arguments that would end with her tossed out into the street and, finally, almost inevitably, to violence. By the year 2000, every day had become a battlefield.

'Why can't I just live here? It'd be easier for us. Easier for the kids.'

He had just come in the door from work and he was already regretting letting her keep a key to the house. 'You know why. You know what you did.'

'Haven't you forgiven me yet?' Her attempts at emotional manipulation fell flat. She could say the words, but her expressions never matched what she was aiming for. 'That was years ago. That was a mistake. I wouldn't do nothing like that again.'

'I know you won't because you ain't moving back into this house.'

Tears would have worked, a quaver in the voice, but Katherine didn't understand sadness or sympathy, she only had rage. Her face went from rosy to scarlet. 'Don't you trust me? After everything I do for you?'

She'd go on and on like this for the rest of the night unless he nipped it in the bud. Once she'd had a good scream to let her frustration out she usually wound down again quick enough. Then it came time to kiss and make up and if there was one thing Kathy was good at, it was kissing and making up. John sometimes thought that those moments were the only reason he had to put up with her at all.

'I ain't a fool, Kathy.' He shook his head. 'I'm never letting you hold nothing over me again. Not ever. When you lose your temper, it doesn't matter what you've promised.'

'Temper?' She growled. 'Temper?! You've never seen me mad, John Price. You think you know fucking everything, don't you? But you know fuck all. You've never seen me angry.'

She sprang up from her seat and tore across the room in a wild charge. John got his hands up in front of his face before she could start slapping. This was all business as usual. She'd wear herself out and have a little cry and show him just how sorry she was. Katherine at her best.

The blows never fell, but something warm and wet was spreading across his chest. Had she thrown a cup of water on him? He nervously moved his arms away and looked down. There was a knife sticking out of his chest, sunk in deep enough to stand proud, but not deep enough to kill him. The tip was scraping on his rib.

He let out a roar and grabbed Katherine by the scruff of her neck. He dragged her to the front door, cast her out into the street, slammed it shut behind her and then sank to the floor, gasping for air. His hands were shaking as he reached up to pluck the knife from his chest. It tumbled from his numb fingers to clatter across the floor beside him. She nearly killed him. If she'd been a half inch down, that knife would have sunk right into his heart. The back door.

He scrambled to his feet, still chill with shock and half-drunk with panic. The back door was sitting slightly ajar to let a breeze through the house, the way it usually was. He could hear the dog bounding about happily in the sunshine just beyond it. It felt like he'd run a mile by the time he reached it and locked it tight.

Not a moment later, he heard a fist thump against it. He'd been right. She was still trying to get in. He did a mental inventory of the house. Dashed around, making sure all the ground floor windows were locked up tight. Then, finally, he staggered, breathless, to slump in his chair in front of the nook in the living room. That had nearly been the end of him. This couldn't go on any longer. It didn't matter what sweet nothings she whispered in his ear, or any of the other things that she could do with that body of hers. If he kept this up, she was going to kill him. He could see that now.

After a fretful night spent worrying that Katherine was out there with a key to his house, a new day dawned. February the 29th. John took himself to the Scone Magistrate's Court a little after dawn and took out a restraining order against Katherine.

All that he had to do was show the court the knife-wound in his chest and they were quick to capitulate.

With that done, he went to work just the same as always, although all of his friends noticed that he had a hunted look about him. By his lunch break, the wound on his chest had oozed through his shirt and he had to seek out a first aid kit to patch it. News of his injury spread through the town like wildfire and all of the people who had turned their back on him because of his relationship with Katherine seemed to come out of the woodwork to offer him solace and advice. To each and every one of them, he said the same thing. 'If I don't show up for work tomorrow, it'll be because she killed me.'

He couldn't bring himself to head home when his shift ended, instead being buoyed along with the rest of the crew to the pub, where he was surrounded by well-wishers and more than one of the town's insufferable gossips, desperate for any fresh details to add to the local legend of Katherine Knight. Every one of his friends offered him a safe bed to sleep in at night, no strings attached, no commentary on his love life, just safety. He turned every one of them down. At first, they thought it was just bravado, that he thought he was tougher than the monster that had sunk a knife into his chest less than a day ago, but eventually, he broke down and told the truth.

'If I'm not there and she shows up ... If she can't get me, she might kill the kids. I can't ... I can't risk that.'

He went home late to discover that the kids were already gone. Katherine had sent them to sleep over at a friend's house and they'd left him a note so he didn't worry. He let out a breath that it felt like he'd been holding all day. His babies were safe.

Less than a minute after that relief, the door rattled in its frame as somebody hammered on it. John froze on the spot. Was it Katherine? There was no way to look out without her seeing him and he hadn't locked the door on his way in. Old habits die hard. Swallowing the cold knot of fear, he strode over to the door and flung it open. He almost collapsed with relief when he saw his neighbour on the doorstep. 'All right, mate?'

The neighbourhood knew all about Katherine Knight and nobody was willing to let her have a good man like John Price without a fight. There wasn't much that they could do to save the man from himself but they could try their best to watch him whilst they could. He spent the rest of the evening lounging around in their garden, sharing bottles of beer and stories of happier times, before he eventually wandered home at eleven to slump into his bed in a drunken stupor.

That was the last time that anyone saw John Price alive.

The Last Supper

Katherine's day had gone in a very different direction to John's. Whilst her shadow stalked his every step, her mind was completely focused on the task at hand. She knew nothing about restraining orders, his mounting desperation to escape her, or anything else that he had done. All that she knew, deep down in the instinctual primordial chaos of her mind, was that he had crossed her and she was going to make him pay, however, she could.

Once she was fairly certain John was gone, she headed over to his house to see the kids. She took her video camera along to make a home movie. She spent the morning filming the children at play, providing a soft, deep-voiced commentary over the whole proceeding, talking about which of the children was to receive which of her belongings when she was gone, talking about who should be given care of her children, if she and John Price should suddenly disappear off the face of the earth. Already, she was trying to construct a narrative. She had no experience with the forensic sciences, she had no knowledge of how cases were composed, but she knew just how to spin a story so that she was the victim, not the perpetrator. She'd been doing it her whole life and doing it so well that, despite everything she had done, she still walked about as a free woman.

With all of the children filmed and accounted for in this video-will, she packed up their things into overnight bags and sent them off to stay with their respective friends for sleepovers. She drove around, dropping them off at their destinations and simmering over the fact that not one parent would come out to greet her. Nobody treated the kids badly—they wouldn't punish them for the sins of their mother—but nobody wanted anything to do with Katherine Knight if they could avoid it.

After the last child was handed off, she drove into town with her very meagre savings in her pocket and bought the fanciest black lingerie that she could find in what she probably thought was the fanciest department store in town. She had never spent so much money on clothing in her life and certainly not on clothing that nobody was ever meant to see outside the bedroom. She wanted to make tonight special.

The rest of the day she spent alone in her little house on MacQueen Street, lost in her thoughts, surrounded by her things, just sitting in silence until the sun went down.

She drove over to St Andrews Street at about eleven o'clock when she was quite certain that John would already have gone to bed. Then, she quietly let herself in. She settled herself in front of the television at first, basking in the normality of it all. This was her home and John was her husband. He had gone to bed early, but now he would be waiting for her. She went through to the bathroom and took a shower, scrubbing herself thoroughly until her skin was as red as her face, then she patted herself dry and dressed up in her new lingerie, admiring herself in the mirror. That John Price, he was a lucky man, to have a wife like her, to do all those things that wives do for their husbands. Sex and cooking, just like her mother used to do for her father. Sex and cooking and cutting. Those were the only things Katherine was good for, but she was so good at them it made up for everything else.

John was lying on his back in bed with the covers flung off in the midsummer heat. His breathing came out in gentle wheezes. He wasn't a snorer like some of the men she'd had. John had been caught young enough by another woman and trained to behave himself. He was used to another person in the bed, so he didn't flinch when the mattress dipped. He didn't stir as she ran her fingers through the hair on his chest. Even when she reached down and stripped off his underwear, he barely responded except to make a little mumble and shift his hips to make it easier for her. John Price, her man, was a creature of habit and she knew just how to use that to her advantage. She worked him with her hand and mouth until he was ready, then climbed on top of him and started to rock her hips. Softly at first, as if she was scared to wake him, then harder and harder, until the fierceness and the intensity of their lovemaking started to shift the bed. Still, she didn't stop, she didn't slow. John's eyes opened slowly, lust-drunk and night-blind. 'Kathy?'

She leaned down and silenced his murmurs with a kiss. Moaning into his mouth. It was like she'd breathed life back into his body. His hands came up and seized her hips, the silk of her lingerie making everything strangely cool and slippery as he fought for a better grip. For more traction.

A little delighted sound slipped out of her as he started to move, not for the pleasure that it brought her—she could bring herself enough pleasure without his involvement—but because it meant he was giving in to her, that he was succumbing without a fight. After the sex, he'd be soft and pliable. She could make him do whatever she wanted, the same as she always had. She just needed to get here and take him in order to win, and now she had.

The bed hammered into the wall over and over, setting her bag of knives jingling above it. They were hanging above his head, right where she'd hung them when she first moved in all those years ago. Of course this house was hers, otherwise, her knives wouldn't be there. Of course this man was hers, or he'd object to her riding him. With a surprised grunt, John finished inside her. She tried to keep moving, to keep this moment going forever, but those strong hands on her hips plucked her right off him and pushed her aside.

John's eyes were open now. Open, awake and aware of what had just happened. There was fear in his eyes. He was scared of her. She'd done that for him, trussed herself up like a Sunday roast, degraded herself for his pleasure, and now he was going to reject her? He was going to toss her off him like she was nothing. Like she was just another one of his whores to be discarded the moment he was done with them. No. She wasn't going to tolerate that. She wasn't going to be thrown out in the street. She wasn't going to be his victim anymore.

Neither of them knew how she got the knife in her hand— that was how quick and instinctive her movements were. One moment she was kneeling there with her face turning scarlet and the next she was lunging forward, the shimmer of fine-edged steel in her hand. It slipped into him so easily that he barely even felt it, so sharp that only the tell-tale wetness that came chasing it out of the wound gave away that he was injured at all. John was still dazed, barely aware of what had happened a moment before and not even slightly conscious that his lung was now collapsing. Her hand snapped forward again, and another little red mouth yawned open on his stomach. The next thrust went in the other side, the blade flipping and twisting in her hand as she shifted its momentum. That one sliced into his liver.

Pain finally cut through his confusion. Pain chased right on its heels by terror. He leapt up off of the bed, too scared to even realise he was dying. He turned heel and ran for the bedroom door. The broad expanse of his back was an easy target for Katherine. She stuck him twice more, cobra-swift. Two more tiny fountains of blood started spraying out his life onto the carpet.

She had been excited before. The dull beginnings of a greater pleasure had built up at the base of her stomach before John had let her down again. But this was better than that; this was better than anything she'd ever felt. Her cheeks ached with smiling, her senses soared. She could smell him, sweat-slick and terrified. She could hear his feeble one-lunged whimpers for help. Wetness clung to her, his sweat, his seed, his blood, she had taken it all from him and now it ran over her skin as she lunged out of the bed after him.

Again and again the knife lashed out, but still, John was too stupid to know he was dead. He ran for the front door, the wash of blood making him too slippery for Katherine to get a good grip. What the mind didn't perceive, the body still couldn't ignore. His limbs were losing strength and his numbed feet were turning under him with each step.

In the hallway, by the front door, he went down. Katherine mounted him the moment he fell. Hammering the blade into his chest and guts as she ground herself against him.

Rage had always been the easiest thing for her, ever since she first let it out. Everything that she saw made her angrier and angrier, every person more loathsome. There wasn't a single waking moment when Katherine wasn't simmering with hatred and resentment for every living creature around her. To let it out like this, to finally be completely honest—it was a revelation.

She knew rage; she could trust rage. Love, which had always been out of reach. Even when she thought that she'd found it, it always seemed to slip through her fingers. She could never tell what a man was thinking or feeling, not really. Her first husband's abandonment had proven that for certain. She never knew what was in any man's heart before this moment, but now she could feel it. Her hand was pressed flat against John's chest to support her weight whilst she stabbed him over and over and she could feel his heart thumping against her, the last desperate throes of a dying animal.

Tapping some reserve of strength found only in the shadow of the valley of death, John bucked her off and grabbed at the door handle. The two of them were more alike than they'd like to admit. Katherine was a creature of habit, too: she'd forgotten to lock the door behind her.

John lunged out into the warm night air, the stars above him shining like pinpricks through the ever-darkening veil that was enveloping him. He opened his mouth to scream for help, but there was no air in his lungs. He tried to crawl out into the street, but her hand was locked like a bear-trap around his ankle. He got one last glimpse of the sky, then she dragged him back inside.

He didn't struggle once he was back in the house. He didn't have the strength any more. The pain was getting more and more distant with every thrust of the knife until he could barely feel them at all. Somewhere between the twentieth and thirtieth stab wound, he died.

Katherine had never been more at peace in her entire life than in the moment that she realised he was dead by her hand. He would never leave her. He would never cross her again. She had her revenge.

Then the reality of it all came crashing down on her: John was dead, she was a murderer, people were going to find out. She was going to get in trouble. She needed to get away. She needed to find someone to blame. She needed to make an excuse. She needed to make it his fault, somehow. With a grimace, she looked down at herself. She needed to have a shower before she did anything else. She looked like she'd spent all day working the line at the meat-works, coated from top to bottom in gore.

After a brief sojourn in the shower to clean off the worst of the mess, Katherine let herself out the back door and drove into town. In the moment, everything had made sense. In the moment, all of the fear and confusion of the modern world had faded away. She had let her primal instincts guide her and she had been elated. Now she was being crushed by the enormity of what she had done. She found an ATM and used John's card, pilfered from his bedside table, to withdraw all of his savings— around a thousand dollars that he'd managed to rebuild after the last time she destroyed his life. It was enough for her to make a

RYAN GREEN

run for it, get set up for a month somewhere to lay low and let the madness that was going to erupt on discovery of John's body pass her by. She already had a bag full of her most prized possessions in the car. She could go now and never look back if she wanted. She could give in to that most primal instinct to flee from danger and see just how far from this nowhere town she could get.

But if she did run, then people would know that she had done it. They would blame her for what she had done. There wouldn't be consequences until they caught up to her, but the whole town—already hissing and whispering about her behind her back—would know that she had killed him for no good reason at all. That she was the bad guy. She couldn't tolerate that. Not when a brief stop at John's house to plant some incriminating evidence would be enough to cover it all up. She'd spent her whole life subject to this town's gossip—she knew just what to say to turn public opinion around.

She pulled up to the house in the early hours of the morning with a dull ache in her bones. All of the excitement had drained out of her body, leaving her feeling hollowed out. The adrenaline rush was over and now she faced the arduous process of cleaning up her own mess.

When she tried to push the door open, it hit against something. With a growl of frustration, she slammed the door into the obstruction over and over, until it was pushed out of the way and she could force her way in. It was only when her footsteps produced a squelch from the carpet that she remembered what she had left lying behind the front door of the house.

She looked down at the heap of meat on the floor. He had done this to her. He had ruined everything. John Price should have loved her like she loved him, but he hadn't. None of them ever had. They weren't men at all. They were swine. Pigs in human skin. Beneath contempt.

Her fingers tangled in his blood-matted hair and she hauled the carcass up to eye level. She spat in his face. 'You. You did this. You did this to me.'

Her knives were still hanging in the bedroom and it only seemed natural to reach for them. All of the confusion that had wracked her only moments before was washed away in the familiar warm rush of anger. He had done this to her and now he had to pay. She'd made the same cuts a million times before on other swine, blade-tip grazing across the spine as she severed the soft tissues and cartilage, easing into the groove between the vertebrae when it came time to separate the head entirely. He was a pig and he deserved to be served up like one.

With a grunt, she lifted his severed head and tossed it into the empty aluminium pot on the stovetop, the one she'd left out to cook him his dinner before he'd thrown her out into the streets over nothing. A splash of water from the tap and some furiously hacked up vegetables joined his head, then she turned on the heat and stalked off. That was how her mother had always prepared pigs-head and that is how she was going to serve it up to his children.

She let out a snort, not unlike a pig's, at that fantasy. Setting John down on the table for his kids to eat, watching those treacherous little cuckoo bastards gobble him down then watch the colour drain out of them when she told them what they'd just consumed.

It still wasn't enough. Not enough for a meal and not enough to sate her other hungers. He had to suffer the way that she'd suffered. She had to strip him of everything that made him John Price. She returned to the rest of his body and continued her work.

If she'd cut a head off a pig a million times, then she'd skinned one a million more. It was tricky, delicate work if you didn't want to score the precious layer of fat underneath. The kind of job that required a more skilful touch than most of the meat-works employees could muster. She made one long, graceful cut along the length of the pelt, then set to separating it from the subcutaneous layers with small, gentle cuts, like she was scraping away the body from inside it more than cutting the hide from the beast. The pot began to bubble and, before long, it smelled just like her mother's kitchen back home. That smell intermingled with the offal and iron of the slaughterhouse, all of Katherine's happy memories, all in one place at last.

She didn't know what to do with his skin once she was finished cutting it from his body, so she hung it from the architrave of the door in the living room and turned back to the meat. A pig's head might make a fine soup and gravy, but there wasn't much eating on it. She really needed more if she was going to provide John's kids with a filling meal. There were a few choice cuts on this particular pig, but the rump had always been her favourite. She sliced each of John's buttocks off with one clean cut a piece, then portioned one in two because she'd taken a little extra meat on that one and didn't want them to cook unevenly. It would be terrible if the kids got food poisoning whilst eating their worthless swine of a father's ass.

She put the meat in to roast, along with a few more handfuls of vegetables. Then, she laid out plates and set the table, scribbling names on a piece of kitchen towel tucked under each plate. 'Beaky' for his daughter Rebecca, and 'Jonathon' for little John.

Finally, she strolled back through to what was left of the corpse and hefted it up into John's favourite seat. It didn't look right. She crossed, then uncrossed the limp cadaver's legs, but it still didn't look like John. Eventually, she got it posed and tucked a bottle of lemonade into the crook of its arm. She started trying to plan out a disguise to cover his corpse with, pawing through his clothes in his room to find a hat or hood so the kids wouldn't notice that their daddy had no head, but it proved useless.

Whilst she waited for the meal to cook, she took a long, slow stroll around the house, smashing every picture that she could find with her bare knuckles. It was only as she ground her hand into the last one, of John and his kids on some sunny afternoon, that she remembered why she had come back to the house to start with. She picked up a pen and a scrap of paper and wrote:

'Time got you back Johathon for rapping my douter. You to Beck for Ross — for Little John. Now play with little Johns Dick, John Price.'

It fell apart a little due to her inability to write in clear English, but the message was essentially conveyed. John Price had been a paedophile, an incestuous child molester who had raped both of his own children and Katherine's, too. It was a baseless accusation, but it was also a lie so hideous that everyone would believe it. Katherine had seen men run out of town on far less evidence than a note from a wife. Her memory, her legend in Aberdeen, would end with her as an avenging angel for the helpless. She would be a folk hero, instead of the bogeyman that the parents of Aberdeen used to threaten their children to sleep.

When the meal was ready, she served two portions of meat out onto the kids' plates, heaped them with vegetables and drizzled them with gravy. It smelled delicious, even though she knew what it was made from.

The third cut of meat lay there in the roasting tin, tempting her with the glisten of rendered fat. One bite would be all that it would take to know for certain if it was as good as it looked. One bite and every part of John Price would belong to her forever. She took that bite, but she couldn't stomach it, spitting it into the sink half chewed and then washing it away. She threw the rest of her portion out into the garden so that the dog could have it when it came home from wherever John had left it.

There was no way that the kids would eat this meal. There was no way that she could trick anyone, let alone the confused and suspicious children of the man she had just murdered. Even this last little attempt at a plan fell apart in the face of reality and, suddenly, it was all too much for Katherine. Her pills were in the kitchen cabinet—the only thing that John had allowed her to keep in his precious house. She fetched every packet of them out and began gulping them down as she dithered around the scenes of her greatest brutality, soaking it all in. The rage was gone and the edges of the world began to darken as she swallowed down packet after packet of sleeping pills, scattering the blister packs across every surface of the house.

In the end, she went back to where the evening had begun, sinking down into the blood-soaked bed and pulling the bedsheet over herself in a makeshift shroud. She had done what she set out to do, and now she could rest.

No Remorse

When John didn't show up for work the next morning, a co-worker was immediately dispatched to check on him. They found the smeared, bloody handprint by his front door. The signs of a body being hauled back inside. The co-worker wasted no time in calling the police and soon the scene was swarming with them.

Katherine was discovered almost immediately, still alive but comatose from her overdose. That was the least disturbing thing that the officers on the scene discovered. It was like a scene from a horror movie. It took the first responders a solid five minutes to work out what the object hanging from the doorway was. It took the lead detective to point out the nose and pubic hair before they could grasp what they were looking at. These were small-town police, unaccustomed to violence of this sort and it took a dreadful toll on every one of them just to observe it. Most left the force soon afterwards, some committed suicide and even the hardiest of them were changed, with those few resilient men suddenly developing an aversion to meat that lasted for years.

They painstakingly pieced together the events of the previous night, measuring the temperature of the boiled head to determine the exact time of John's death.

John's body was taken to the coroner's office, where it was discovered that he had suffered thirty-seven separate stab wounds prior to his death. It was abundantly clear that whoever had killed him was an expert skinner, because the incisions that had been made were so perfect that, when the autopsy was over, the coroner was able to stitch John back into his skin, leaving him looking almost as he did when he was alive.

It was two days later that Katherine woke up. The police were on hand to question her, but they quickly discovered that the hardened killer, whom they thought was in their clutches, had severe mental health problems. From the very beginning of her questioning, she claimed to remember nothing about the events of the night, but she was careful to cast doubt on any claim that she was responsible for John's death, talking at great length about how much she loved him. Were there no other witnesses to the rest of Katherine's life, it is possible that she would have convinced the police of either her innocence or insanity to a degree that she would avoid conviction, but that was not the case. When the police began canvassing the area for any witnesses, they were approached by a delegation of the townsfolk of Aberdeen who begged them to ensure that Katherine never got out. Every person in Aberdeen lived in fear of her and they dreaded what new heights of horror she could achieve if she were set loose again.

Her trial began surprisingly quickly following her arrest, with the courts desperate to get through it before news of the horrific details had spread too far and compromised too many jurors. Even as it was, it was almost impossible to get jurors to sit for her trial. The few who hadn't already heard rumours about the atrocity had the scene of the crime described to them before they took up their position on the jury, and the threat of having to see pictures of her victim was sufficient that many of them begged off. It was with some relief that the judge was able to dismiss the jury after her lawyers had entered a guilty plea.

Sadly, this plea came with some strings attached. Katherine would admit to the lesser crime of manslaughter in exchange for a reduced sentence. The judge, Justice O'Keefe, refused the plea outright. This was one of the most horrific crimes he had ever heard of and there was no way that he was ever letting the perpetrator walk free again.

The plea was switched to 'not guilty' and the jury trial began again in earnest, but before it could progress too far, O'Keefe dragged it to a halt once more, sending Katherine off for a psychological evaluation to prove that she was competent to enter a not-guilty plea, rather than an insanity defence.

It was during these assessments that the formal diagnosis of BPD was finally attached to Katherine, even though some of her old carers came out of the woodwork to deny it. With the BPD diagnosis, Katherine was able to claim that she had been suffering a period of disassociation during the gruesome acts of March the first, explaining her missing memories. Her lawyers ran with the diagnosis, committing to several bouts of theatrics to convince the jury that Katherine was not culpable—or at least, not fully culpable—for her own actions. The largest of these theatrical events was when Katherine begged to be excused during the descriptions of her crimes, and when that was refused, launching herself into a hysterical fit that ended with her being sedated.

Despite all of these tricks, the jury saw through her and she was found guilty of premeditated murder, along with lesser crimes associated with her treatment of John's body. The judge sentenced her to life in prison, with a special addendum added to her file: 'never to be released.' This essentially denied her any hope of parole, making her the first woman in Australia to ever receive such a harsh sentence.

Mulawa High-Security Prison has been Katherine Knight's home since the day of her sentencing, but it is difficult to punish a person who lives like an animal at the best of times. A typical day for Katherine begins at seven when she is woken by the four guards who will serve as her escort for the day. She eats breakfast at a table away from the other inmates and is then walked to her job in the prison's earphone factory. She is manacled to her workstation, out of reach of any other inmates, and sets to work assembling the tiny pieces by hand for up to six hours, depending on her shift. Her work ethic and skill is widely praised by the prison staff and she commands the highest wage in the entire factory, but those aren't the only traits that the guards comment on.

The other inmates call her, 'The Nanna,' and she is widely-considered to run the female side of the institution. When there is a dispute between inmates, she is called in to resolve it, and whatever her judgement is pronounced to be, is taken as law. Even when there is a dispute between the guards and the inmates, she is usually referred to. Everyone is terrified of her and she basks in the kind of respect that she had always dreamed of.

A prolific artist, her single person cell is filled to bursting with craft projects, knitting, crochet, drawings, paintings and pottery. It is her private space that nobody is allowed to enter, whether they be inmate or guard. Indeed, the only comfort that Katherine is truly denied is a cell-mate. It has been decided that there is too great a risk to the life of anyone put into a domestic situation with her to justify the savings that might be made.

Her artwork decorates the visitors' and guards' sections of the prison, with many pieces being sold off with her approval to help fund some of the education and entertainment programmes on offer. Katherine is very careful never to sign any of her original artwork, despite basking in the attention that they bring her. She does not want any true crime fans out in the world buying her art simply because she was the one who made it.

Any friends or family have long since abandoned Katherine to her fate, with only a single exception. Whilst her children, co-workers, parents, and brothers have turned their backs on the murderess, her twin, Joy, still comes to visit whenever she is able, riding the bus for hours to get to the prison.

In 2006, she launched an appeal against her sentence, claiming that it was too harsh for the single murder that she had committed. A panel of three of New South Wales' most prominent judges gathered to review the case and promptly ratified her original sentence. Katherine had never shown any sign of remorse for her actions and, without remorse, there can be no basis for parole under the Australian system. It is for this reason that a guilty plea is often preferable to a prisoner than a not-guilty one, even when a reduction in time to be served is not offered.

In the time since her arrest, more accounts had been gathered about her personal dealings that had helped to seal her fate. In particular, a series of conversations with her brother, Kenneth and niece, Tracy, when she said, 'I am going to kill Pricey and I am going to get away with it. I'll get away with it because I'll make out I'm mad.'

Justice McClellan responded to her appeal with one additional statement, which seems to reflect the views of everyone in Australia. 'This was an appalling crime, almost beyond contemplation in a civilized society.'

The 'primitive intelligence' that drove Katherine Knight to commit her heinous crimes against her fellow man exists inside each and every one of us. Buried under layers of guilt, conditioning, education and intelligence, there is a primal part to every psyche driven exclusively by raw emotion and need. In a narcissistic psychopath like Katherine Knight, civilisation is a mask to be worn over this primal reality. The truth that others are different from them, that people have depth and understanding beyond what the psychopath thinks and feels, is impossible to comprehend. It is as though the psychopath is completely alone in the world, with no friend or ally, and reversion to savagery is the only way that they can ensure their own survival. For a woman like that, remorse would be a display of weakness that others might exploit. The full depth of her emotional state is always going to be beyond the psychologists and criminologists who pore over her crimes and profile because even if she possesses complexity beyond that which she displays, she lacks the tools required to communicate with others. Something that decades in relative isolation within a prison certainly has not improved.

It is possible that Katherine Knight felt bad about what she did to John Price, just as it is possible that the lioness feels bad as she tears out the throat from a gazelle. The unpleasant truth is that the predator's feelings do not matter in the face of the material reality of their actions. And, in the case of Katherine Knight, those actions are now considered to be one of the worst crimes to have ever been committed in Australian history

Want More?

Did you enjoy *Man-Eater* and want some more True Crime?

YOUR FREE BOOK IS WAITING

From bestselling author Ryan Green

There is a man who is officially classed as **"Britain's most dangerous prisoner"**

The man's name is Robert Maudsley, and his crimes earned him the nickname **"Hannibal the Cannibal"**

This free book is an exploration of his story...

★★★★★ *"Ryan brings the horrifying details to life. I can't wait to read more by this author!"*

Get a free copy of **Robert Maudsley: Hannibal the Cannibal** when you sign up to join my Reader's Group.

www.ryangreenbooks.com/free-book

Every Review Helps

If you enjoyed the book and have a moment to spare, I would really appreciate a short review on Amazon. Your help in spreading the word is gratefully received and reviews make a huge difference to helping new readers find me. Without reviewers, us self-published authors would have a hard time!

Type in your link below to be taken straight to my book review page.

US	geni.us/ManEUS
UK	geni.us/ManEUK
Australia	geni.us/ManEAUS
Canada	geni.us/ManECA

Thank you! I can't wait to read your thoughts.

About Ryan Green

Ryan Green is a true crime author who lives in Herefordshire, England with his wife, three children, and two dogs. Outside of writing and spending time with his family, Ryan enjoys walking, reading and windsurfing.

Ryan is fascinated with History, Psychology and True Crime. In 2015, he finally started researching and writing his own work and at the end of the year, he released his first book on Britain's most notorious serial killer, Harold Shipman.

He has since written several books on lesser-known subjects, and taken the unique approach of writing from the killer's perspective. He narrates some of the most chilling scenes you'll encounter in the True Crime genre.

You can sign up to Ryan's newsletter to receive a free book, updates, and the latest releases at:

WWW.RYANGREENBOOKS.COM

More Books by Ryan Green

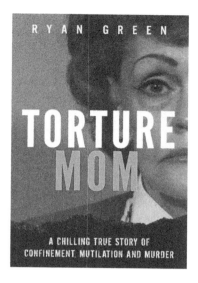

In July 1965, teenagers Sylvia and Jenny Likens were left in the temporary care of Gertrude Baniszewski, a middle-aged single mother and her seven children.

The Baniszewski household was overrun with children. There were few rules and ample freedom. Sadly, the environment created a dangerous hierarchy of social Darwinism where the strong preyed on the weak.

What transpired in the following three months was both riveting and chilling. The case shocked the entire nation and would later be described as "The single worst crime perpetuated against an individual in Indiana's history".

More Books by Ryan Green

On 29th February 2000, John Price took out a restraining order against his girlfriend, Katherine Knight. Later that day, he told his co-workers that she had stabbed him and if he were ever to go missing, it was because Knight had killed him.

The next day, Price didn't show up for work.

A co-worker was sent to check on him. They found a bloody handprint by the front door and they immediately contacted the police. The local police force was not prepared for the chilling scene they were about to encounter.

Price's body was found in a chair, legs crossed, with a bottle of lemonade under his arm. He'd been decapitated and skinned. The "skin-suit" was hanging from a meat hook in the living room and his head was found in the kitchen, in a pot of vegetables that was still warm. There were two plates on the dining table, each had the name of one of Price's children on it.

She was attempting to serve his body parts to his children.

More Books by Ryan Green

In 1902, at the age of 11, Carl Panzram broke into a neighbour's home and stole some apples, a pie, and a revolver. As a frequent troublemaker, the court decided to make an example of him and placed him into the care of the Minnesota State Reform School. During his two-year detention, Carl was repeatedly beaten, tortured, humiliated and raped by the school staff.

At 15-years old, Carl enlisted in the army by lying about his age but his career was short-lived. He was dishonourably discharged for stealing army supplies and was sent to military prison. The brutal prison system sculpted Carl into the man that he would remain for the rest of his life. He hated the whole of mankind and wanted revenge.

When Carl left prison in 1910, he set out to rob, burn, rape and kill as many people as he could, for as long as he could. His campaign of terror could finally begin and nothing could stand in his way.

More Books by Ryan Green

In 1861, the police of a rural French village tore their way into the woodside home of Martin Dumollard. Inside, they found chaos. Paths had been carved through mounds of bloodstained clothing, reaching as high as the ceiling in some places.

The officers assumed that the mysterious maid-robber had killed one woman but failed in his other attempts. Yet, it was becoming sickeningly clear that there was a vast gulf between the crimes they were aware of and the ones that had truly been committed.

Would Dumollard's wife expose his dark secret or was she inextricably linked to the atrocities? Whatever the circumstances, everyone was desperate to discover whether the bloody garments belonged to some of the 648 missing women.

Free True Crime Audiobook

Sign up to Audible and use your free credit to download this collection of twelve books. If you cancel within 30 days, there's no charge!

WWW.RYANGREENBOOKS.COM/FREE-AUDIOBOOK

"Ryan Green has produced another excellent book and belongs at the top with true crime writers such as M. William Phelps, Gregg Olsen and Ann Rule" –**B.S. Reid**

"Wow! Chilling, shocking and totally riveting! I'm not going to sleep well after listening to this but the narration was fantastic. Crazy story but highly recommend for any true crime lover!" –**Mandy**

"Torture Mom by Ryan Green left me pretty speechless. The fact that it's a true story is just...wow" –**JStep**

"Graphic, upsetting, but superbly read and written" –**Ray C**

WWW.RYANGREENBOOKS.COM/FREE-AUDIOBOOK

Made in the USA
Coppell, TX
16 December 2024

42593881R00083